3356   4/49   5/6

D1334561

BUCKINGHAMSHIRE FOOTPATHS

Books by J. H. B. Peel

Poetry
TIME TO GO
IN THE COUNTRY
MERE ENGLAND
FROST AT MIDNIGHT

Essays
TO BE BRIEF
SMALL CALENDARS

Travel
BUCKINGHAMSHIRE FOOTPATHS
THE CHILTERNS: A VISION OF ENGLAND

AVENUE NEAR WESCOTT

BUCKINGHAMSHIRE
FOOTPATHS

By

J. H. B. PEEL

LONDON
CHATERSON LTD
5 JOHNSON'S COURT, FLEET STREET, E.C.4

This is a CROSS-COUNTRY BOOK. *Other Titles in this series are* CHILTERN FOOTPATHS *by Annan Dickson (fifteenth thousand),* FOOTPATHS OF THE KENT–SUSSEX BORDER *by Joseph Braddock,* COUNTRY OF THE THAMES *by Annan Dickson.*

THIS BOOK IS PRODUCED IN COMPLETE CONFORMITY WITH THE AUTHORIZED ECONOMY STANDARDS

First published 1949

PRINTED IN GREAT BRITAIN BY RICHARD CLAY AND COMPANY, LTD., BUNGAY, SUFFOLK.

Carissimis istis amicis atque locis inter quos et
puer et juvenis felix eram datus est hic liber.

For me, why should I wish to roam?
This spot is my paternal home,
It is my pleasant heritage;
My father many a happy year
Spread here his careless blossoms, here
Attained a good old age.

—WILLIAM WORDSWORTH.

CONTENTS

The photographs were selected and taken specially for this book by the author and Mr. Raoul de Normanville, of Stephen Foster Ltd., The Studio, Studham, Bedfordshire. With additional photographs on pages 4, 44–5, 46, 47, 90, by the Mustograph Agency ; on pages 17, 74, 98, 113, by Mr. E. W. Tattersall ; on page 76, by Fox Photos Ltd. ; on page 10, by Mr. A. Harold Bastin ; on page 76 (*top*), by Mr. E. C. Mansell ; and on the jacket by Dorien Leigh, Ltd.

LIST OF ILLUSTRATIONS

WILLEN CHURCH

CHAPTER ONE

Getting to Know Buckinghamshire

I was travelling once with a north-countryman to whom, the conversation turning upon the English scene, I remarked that my own home lay on the outskirts of a small village in a remote part of the Chilterns, where the hills were not far short of a thousand feet above the sea: to which my companion replied, that nowhere south of the Pennines were any real hills, and nowhere within one hundred miles of London was any real country.

Notwithstanding that the northern border of this County merges with Northamptonshire—a very considerable distance indeed from London—and that the hamlet of Little Hampden, which I see from my window, lies three miles from any shop or motor bus—notwithstanding this, my fellow-traveller returned into his native fastness with a conviction that God had made the country indeed, but only north of the Pennines. What a Swiss mountaineer would have said of his Grampians, I do not know.

I cite this imperfectly-educated provincial in order to introduce immediately, and to dispose of forthwith, the misconceived notion of Buckinghamshire as an immense Metroland. Let it be understood at once that some parts of the County near to London have indeed become mere Metroland. The Londonward side of Amersham, for example, is marred beyond mending. Gems exist there, it is true, and many of them within eighteen miles of the City, but the area as a whole is tainted now by the unwholesome fumes of Cobbett's great wen, and an urban *Ichabod* is writ large

THE VIEW FROM PRESTWOOD

upon many a "sweet especial rural scene". We have ravished a lovely corner of England that in a civilized nation would have been preserved with at least as much care as now we lavish upon criminals and the insane.

It is not my purpose to describe this area, nor to gloss over it. It exists, forever unredeemable, and must be faced. It has its own devotees, whom only the arrogant fool will seek to assail. People who relish that sort of scenery will relish that sort of scenery. My purpose, rather, is to re-explore the antique and unsullied Buckinghamshire, excluding the Chilterns, for they have been described in a Companion Volume of this series.

To this end I have chosen seven walks around Aylesbury, Buckingham, and Newport Pagnell, amid scenery that I dwelt in as a boy, and have known closely and loved dearly throughout my life. It is not possible to mention every place within this sector, and I have therefore contented myself by describing closely a few typical walks that may encourage the wayfarer to plan others with the help of map and this introduction.

At this point I would emphasize that the book is not—because it was never intended to be—a comprehensive introduction to the County's flora and fauna, antiquities, geology, culture, rainfall, or economic life. I have written elsewhere, and in greater detail, of the historic associations of Buckinghamshire, and in a vein more likely to commend itself to those readers who relish the *minutiae* of local history. In this book we are in holiday mood, and shall content ourselves by mapping routes and by nodding as it were to the interesting objects that flank them. For this reason, therefore, we shall bestride Grimm's Dyke without perplexing ourselves as to the identity of the Rhenish, or Belgic, or Celtic tribe that may have constructed it; and while admiring Hampdenleaf Wood, we shall not concern ourselves with John Hampden's attitude towards the Sheriff who served upon him the famous levy.

Lest any man still cling to the parochial superstition of my Grampian friend, I may state here—since the matter has a direct bearing upon this book—that many parts of Buckinghamshire are extremely remote. Bletchley, alone of all the places here cited, lies along a major main railway. Some of the hamlets and footpaths to be described are several miles from a station, and one or two of them are more than an hour's walk from the twice-weekly motor-bus. The majority, however, are near to a railway or motor-bus: and I have described the best approach to these, in the appropriate chapter.

The region to be explored, then, is not likely to be known by many people. It will, I believe, prove novel to most

JOHN HAMPDEN'S STATUE AT AYLESBURY

readers, and should therefore be welcome also, if only for that reason; although, as I hope to show, both the countryside and its peoples are valuable and in their own right full of beauty.   I am describing a new and a homely dish for the delight of those to whom caviare and tinned beans are alike stale and over-rated.

Before we proceed to explore these footpaths, a word or two about Buckinghamshire itself will refresh some memories, and may be news to many more.   Buckinghamshire is what the journalists would call the thirty-fourth smallest (or largest) County in England.   At its northernmost point, beyond Olney, where the poet Cowper lived, it borders upon Northamptonshire, and is nearly seventy miles from the centre of London.

The County is bounded on the south and south-west by Berkshire; on the west by Oxfordshire; on the north and north-west by Northamptonshire; on the north-east by Bedfordshire; on the east by Bedfordshire and Hertfordshire; and on the south-east by Middlesex.   In area it is roughly 750 square miles, and has not changed in outline since the village of Ibstone, which used to be in Oxfordshire, became a part of Buckinghamshire.   From north to south—from Olney to a point near Windsor Castle—the County is 53 miles long.   Its average breadth is only 18 miles; at its widest, 27 miles.

Of the four principal rivers—the Ouse, the Thame, the Colne, and the Thames—our walks will encounter only the first two.   The Ouse is formed by two streams on the outskirts of the town of Buckingham.   One of these streams rises in Northamptonshire, the other in Oxfordshire.   The river itself passes Stony Stratford, Newport Pagnell, and Olney, whence it enters Bedfordshire, at the hamlet of Branfield.

The Thame—which we shall encounter near Dinton and

B

Aylesbury—is the harvest of many small streams. It flows past Thame and Aylesbury in a south-westerly direction, to join the Isis at Dorchester, where the Isis becomes the Thames.

We shall meet a third river also, the Ousel, on our walks between Sympson and Newport Pagnell. The Ousel is a small river (in places, a stream only) forming the Bedfordshire–Buckinghamshire border from Eaton Bray to Leighton Buzzard. It enters our County near Stoke Hammond, a pretty village athwart canal and railway, whence it flows through Water Eaton and Fenny Stratford to Newport Pagnell. It is a little over 31 miles long.

Even to-day, Buckinghamshire is primarily—I would

THE CANAL AT GREAT LINFORD

say, almost entirely—a farming county; for, except at Slough, which is now merely a suburb of London, there is no town of even the second rank; and a census taken between the two wars revealed that the majority of the population were engaged in farming.

The soil of Buckinghamshire, which must be of interest to everyone who is out for something fuller than a mere hike, may be divided, for general description, into three sorts—each overlapping the others, it is true, but each predominating in its own area. These are chalk, deep sand, and loam-and-clay.

Chalk predominates in the Chiltern Hills, which are beyond the scope of this book; deep sand predominates along the borders of Bedfordshire, near Broughton, Wavendon, and the three Brickhills; the mixture of rich loam and stiff clay predominates in the northern half of the County, which is especially our province. It is interesting to note that—until the late war unsettled our economy—nearly half of the farms were arable, with a high acreage of grassland. Buckinghamshire stock were always noted, and the saying " Buckinghamshire bread and beef " was common until we invented refrigeration, and thereby gave away our meat trade to New Zealand, Australia, and the Argentine.

And since we are English folk, our national characteristics not yet wholly eliminated by Orders in Council, we may notice also the love (you may prefer to dub it the addiction) of Buckinghamshire men for sport. We have several packs of foxhounds in our territory, as well as an excellent farmers' drag. The Old Berkeley Beagles do good work hereabouts, and in the north of the County are some otterhounds. I am told that the tender feelings of the fox have come to the forefront nowadays—save among those farmers whose chickens and lambs they maul—and that hunting may prove an unpopular topic of conversation.

IN THE SMITHY, GREAT HAMPDEN

The fact remains, as Trollope reminded us in his *Auto-biography*, that there are few ways, better than hunting, for learning the lie of the land—and the temperature of the slime in its ditches. Not many folk can afford to hunt nowadays, and one at least of our packs is subsidized from Threadneedle Street and the Stock Exchange; but many a farmer goes without, in order to keep one hunter; and it is the nicest sight in the world to see these bulwarks of the chase as they forgather at the meet. We know nothing of the urban snobbery of some Shire Packs. I can turn out in old boots and a rat-catcher jacket, and the Master will still salute me. Finally, all rowing men will acknowledge that Henley—which is flanked by Bucking-hamshire beech hills—is the oarsman's Mecca.

Various explanations have been offered of the origin of its name, the most likely being *Boc-ing-ham*, meaning the *ham*, or home, of the *ings*, or sons, of one *Boc*, who settled here in early Saxon times, very probably from a Germanic tribe. The abbreviation of this melodious name into Bucks is not, as one might suppose, an instance of contemporary slackness, but was invented by medieval monks who, in order to save time while writing the names of counties, used as a rule the first four letters of each name, adding an *s* at the end, itself an abbreviation of the word *shire*. This *shire*, in its turn, was a corruption of the Saxon word *share*, meaning a division. Edward the Elder built several forts and caused a number of men from each division to hold the defences. Hence the division, or area, from which men were summoned to hold the fort of Buckingham, was called Buckinghamshire.

The northern half of Buckinghamshire is curiously ill-served by railways and main roads, and has therefore re-tained a relatively high degree of civilization. Cosy cafés, palaces-of-dance, super-cinemas, and other attributes of pro-

A BUCKINGHAMSHIRE BODGER'S "SHOP"

gress are here, as the Bible puts it, not. Various railways
do indeed dissect the district—notably from Aylesbury,
Bletchley, and Buckingham—yet these are "one-eyed,
blinking" sort of things, crusted with a venerable hoar:
quaint in themselves and, although efficient, romantical
also; much given to sojourning at lonely halts; and
noticeably self-sufficient in so far as the drivers are not
averse from opening their own level-crossings, nor the fire-
men from collecting the passengers' fare. Ironically
enough, a journey along such a railway will restore to some
travellers a sense of lost leisure, and a pristine repose, that
are nowadays absent from the highways, where hundreds of
travellers are killed or maimed every week.

Lacking, then, a system of swift and co-ordinated transport, and being moreover devoid of major mineral resources,

this blessed corner of England has no large town and is still predominantly agricultural. Buckingham itself is not more than an elongated village, and Newport Pagnell is not even elongated. Bletchley, it is true, is a major railway junction, foredoomed to become a satellite town of 60,000 persons, but we need not visit the place. There is not one big town throughout Buckinghamshire, and (unless we include Slough, which is London) no centre of commerce or industry. This fact you will applaud or lament according to your disposition.

Antiquities abound here—buildings, weapons, pottery —and in the Whaddon Chase country, near the Northamptonshire border, coins of the reign of Cymbeline have been unearthed. Little Brickhill, on the Watling Street, was the great Roman camp of *Magiovintum*; Saxon graves have been found at Dinton, in the Vale of Aylesbury; and at Newport Pagnell an entire Saxon cemetery was discovered. It is neither possible nor desirable to cite these matters at length. They will be mentioned as they occur, in the course of each walk.

Of Buckinghamshire's literary associations, however, it is necessary to speak at some length, for they are unique among the counties of England. Milton lived for many years at Chalfont and at Horwood ; at the latter place he composed his two poems to joy and melancholy. William Cowper lived near Olney for thirty years, where he wrote his greatest poems, among them that formidable epic of male spinsterhood, *The Task*. At the inn of Grendon Underwood Shakespeare wrote some of his gayest poetry, and tradition says, with some sense of truth, that Dogberry and Verges were Grendon constables. Edmund Waller was a Buckinghamshire poet. Shelley lived at Marlow, and Burke near to Beaconsfield. Disraeli spent his boyhood at Bradenham, and the happiest years of his manhood at Hughenden.   Gray, as we all know, conceived his *Elegy* in the churchyard of Stoke Poges, and Robert Louis Stevenson thought well enough of the County to have spent some time in it and to praise it.   At " The Pink and Lily ", by Loosley Row, young Rupert Brooke was a regular visitor, and John Masefield lived for a time in Great Hampden, where, I believe, he wrote a great part of *Reynard the Fox*, together with some of his best sonnets.

At risk of tiring some readers, and alienating others, I shall interpolate here a little of the historical background of Buckinghamshire, because I believe that such a background, once it has been acquired, can enrich the wayfarer's exploration of the countryside.   I would go further, and say that no man can fully enjoy these villages unless he knows something of their story—unless, that is to say, he knows how, and why, their wonderful church architecture arose and with the Reformation declined; unless he understands that England was once a farming community, first as exporters of wool, then as exporters of wool and woollen goods, and finally not as farmers at all, in any living sense, but as makers of goods.   The wayfarer must remember that these Buckinghamshire villages were at one time ruled by the lord, then controlled by the squire, and at last handed over to Parliament and local councils.   He must recollect also that each of these Buckinghamshire villages was once self-sufficient, producing its own food, weaving and tailoring its own clothes, having each its own farrier, cooper, carpenter, wheelwright, and cobbler.   This self-sufficiency continued, in lessening degree, to within living memory, and has not yet wholly disappeared, since it is only within living memory that transport has become swift enough, and sufficiently extensive, to allow a national interchange of commodities.   As our wayfarer enters each village church—perhaps merely for the shade's sake, or to

MONUMENT TO
JOHN HAMPDEN,
PRESTWOOD

AN UNUSUAL WAR
MEMORIAL

shelter from a shower—he must not be perplexed by their size and number and beauty, but must recall that they were built by, and for, men to whom God was real, and faith a matter of everyday concern; nor will he be wide of the mark if he supposes that faith endured—again, with lessening intensity—until living memory, when Darwin and Doubt superseded it among the upper, and Pictures and Pleasure among the lower, stratum of society.

Remembering, furthermore, that Feudalism was based upon personal obligation towards a superior, our modern wayfarer will know that (although such obligations began to be commuted for cash payment, so early as the twelfth century) such a notion of personal obligation persists in some English villages even to this day and against the spirit of organized labour and absentee landlordism. There are Halls and Courts and Manors in Buckinghamshire to-day—and throughout the kingdom—where the owner is owner also of the entire village or hamlet; where he is loved—yes, loved—by his tenants, as Sir Roger de Coverley was loved by *his* tenants; where he is served by retainers who spend their lives in his employ gladly. These things may not endure for very long, and it is therefore a matter of interest to observe them while they are with us, that we may recount them accurately and at first hand to our grandchildren.

Last of all, a word about reference books; with which my interpolation shall end. The first and greatest of these is Domesday Book—a collection of facts that is not at all intimidating, despite its academic associations. Copies of the entries for this County can be had from the Buckinghamshire Archaeological Society, at the Museum, Aylesbury, for a few shillings. In Domesday we have a picture of English villages as they were at the time of Edward the Confessor; at the time of the Conquest; and toward the end of the eleventh century. Domesday was drawn up by

William the Conqueror for one purpose only—to help him reassess taxation, and learn the names of tax-dodgers. It is not a complete survey of the kingdom—parts of the north are ignored, and parts of the west have their own survey—nor is it a complete picture of village life; but it does give the size of each village, its lord, the number of its ponds, mills, stock, farm implements, tenants, and several other details.   Copies of the Pipe Rolls for Buckinghamshire can also be had from the Museum, and these furnish much intimate history of a later phase of the Middle Ages.

From the many hundreds of guide-books and monographs, two seem outstanding; the first, on account of its own historic importance; the second, for its succinct retailing of picturesque news.   *The History and Antiquities*

EARLY SPRING AT MANOR FARM, LITTLE HAMPDEN

of the County of Buckingham, by George Lipscomb, is the senior survey of the County, published one hundred years ago; *History and Topography of Buckinghamshire*, by James Joseph Sheahan, appeared in 1862. It is, of course, out of date in many ways, but much of its information stands to-day and the book itself offers a vivid picture of the County as it used to be.

For readers who prefer to take their history with jam, and *via* a more personal route, there are the classic *Memoirs of the Verney Family During the Civil Wars*, by Frances P. Verney, 1892; and in the same vein, *Shardeloes Papers of the* 17*th and* 18*th Century*, by G. Eland (Oxford University Press, 1947). These two books concern respectively the north and the south of Buckinghamshire, the Vale and the Chilterns, and each gives a picture of the old ways, tinder indeed to the historic imagination. *The Victoria History of the County of Buckingham* (1905–8) covers many aspects of its subject and offers the last word on botany, geology, history, economics, and topography. All of the books I have cited can be had of a good public library.

County architecture will be mentioned as it occurs in each walk; and here it must suffice to say that the half-timbered cottages of north Buckinghamshire are a unique feature of the landscape, and the envy of American millionaires, who indeed have caused several of them to be uprooted, and re-assembled in the empire of our forefathers across the Atlantic.

Many Buckinghamshire people come of Saxon origin, as their surnames suggest, and a recent survey has shown that Vale people are darker than Chiltern folk. In the eleventh century the population of the County was not more than 30,000. To-day the hybrid factory-site of Slough is more populous than that. North Buckinghamshire has always been thinly peopled. The population of

Creslow, for example, was six in Queen Elizabeth's reign; that of Tattenhoe, eighteen; of Ilmer, fifty-one. Even to-day there are many hamlets with a population of less than one hundred. More surprising is the fact that a twentieth-century census showed one-fifth of the population to be engaged in farming. Eight hundred persons were still making lace by hand, many of them within their own cottages.

Finally, what are the general characteristics of the scene that we are to explore? What does the region look like? Is it hilly, or flat? Wooded, or treeless? Well-watered, or dry? The answer lies mid-way between these extremes, for Buckinghamshire—except in the Chiltern Hills—is a gently-rolling landscape, pleasant, sequestered, seemingly entering

A CORNER OF WHITCHURCH

upon, or emerging out of, a deep sleep.   Our sector lacks
the beech-clad slopes of the Chiltern country, but
nowhere, not even in the Vale of Aylesbury, is the land
uniformly flat.   Brill, for instance, stands 800 feet above
sea-level; from Bow Brickhill there is a splendid view across
the valley of the Ouse, deep into Bedfordshire and
Northamptonshire; and from many a lane around Buckingham you may see hillocks of oak and elm and ash, quiet in
the sunlight; or forest, river, and meadow double-lovely
from a distance.   Truly the men of this County may say:

> Our Fens we have, where lonely Cowper lived,
> beside the Ouse, upon that lowly plain
> through Whaddon, Fenny Stratford, Milton Keynes,
> and little Sympson's little stripling hills.
> By Summer Heath the lanes are carved so deep
> that Devon men might dream themselves at home,
> and Hardy's bitter Egdon looms again
> at Russell's Water, where a man may peer
> full-circle, and discern no dwelling place.

I believe that its remoteness will seem to many visitors
to be its principal charm.   Sussex is lovely, Kent is lovely,
even Surrey and Hertfordshire and Bedfordshire have their
homely charms, but nowhere within them will the wayfarer
experience that sense of peace, which is an Absolute of life,
more securely than in the deepest countryside of north
Buckinghamshire.   In Surrey and Sussex and Kent an
electric train has brought London to the Downs and
amid hop-fields; but in north Buckinghamshire there is
no such system of rapid railways.   It will take you longer
to travel from Ilmer to Gayhurst than from London to
Birmingham; and as for going from Mursley to Walton,
I have no ideas at all on the subject; I rather think you
would have to walk there.   In the other Home Counties,
moreover, most of the villages are linked to the towns by

motor omnibus, but large tracts of north Buckinghamshire are even to-day isolated from the towns—indeed, Newport Pagnell and Olney are scarcely towns at all. If, for example, you were a Drayton Parslow man, you would walk no doubt into Winslow for your tobacco, but in Winslow you would find simply a farming community. North Buckinghamshire is wholly an unsophisticated county. It has nothing in it like a Tenterden, a Guildford, or a Welwyn. And the beauty of it is, I see no threat to this state of affairs. Who, after all, would benefit from a motor-bus between Milton Keynes and Woughton-on-the-Green?

No man who knows Buckinghamshire will quarrel with me when I say that here is a country of repose and moderation; not flamboyant nor startling, but studded with many vistas of field, farmstead, and church. To the quiet man who in these unquiet times is braced and made whole again by contact with things strong and steadfast and English, his County, which happens also to be my own home, is a very haven, in which he will find, not escape nor mere distraction, but the still, small voice of reality, cool and unwavering and melodious amid the vast mirage of contemporary arrogance and haste.

CHAPTER TWO

FROM FENNY STRATFORD, THROUGH SYMPSON, TO THE
   THREE BRICKHILLS AND LEIGHTON BUZZARD.   (ABOUT
   9 MILES)

FENNY STRATFORD or Bletchley are the starting-points of
our first walk.   At Fenny Stratford is a branch line from
Bletchley into Bedford, and at the cross-roads in the
village you may take the motor-bus along the Watling
Street, past Staple Hall, to Denbigh Bridge, something
over a mile to the north-west of the village.

Denbigh Bridge is of some interest, for a plaque there
tells us that the railway from London formerly ended by
" The Denbigh Arms ", under the shadow of the bridge,
and that passengers to the north of England had thence to
proceed by coach to the next tract of railway, which was
owned by another company.   In time the two companies
became the London and North-Western Railway, which in
its turn joined with others to become the old London,
Midland, and Scottish line out of Euston.   " The Denbigh
Arms ", therefore, now a remote beer-house, was at one
time a major coaching inn, well known to all those travellers
and busy industrialists of the last century who gave us
Birmingham and Manchester and other gems of *kultur* and
the good life.

A few yards beyond " The Denbigh Arms " is a signpost
pointing rightward in the direction of Sympson, but any
motorist who is deceived by it will find his machine in some
discomfort, for the way is no more than a reinforced cart-
track; indeed, when we were children, we christened it
Blackberry Lane, from many such expeditions there with
our grandfather.

I have an especial affection for this lane, since the best part of my boyhood was spent at Staple Hall, not far away from it; a pleasant country house that once had its orchard and fruit-garden and a fine sweep of lawn, but is to-day given over to the builders.   On this lane, however, you need have no fears for the present, nor for the future either, but only a tempered regret for a past that, despite its manifold shortcomings, not only seemed to have, but did in fact possess, many good things that now we lack.

I see no change in this lane as the years flow quietly by— unless indeed it be that the gypsies, who encamp along the furzy banks, have grown sluttish with the times, and nowadays take no trouble to remove their litter, so that tin cans, burned-out kettles, newspapers, and the pink parts of feminine underwear, are now to be found hanging from profuse blackberry bushes, or broadcast willy-nilly in dells and upon mole-hills.   Yet, for all that, Blackberry Lane remains full of adventure and of small surprises that never happen—a mile of remote peace and a rare solitude.   The way is lovely in all weathers, and for kindness' sake has the knack of adapting itself to all moods.   It is lovely in spring, when grass is green and sappy; and it is lovely in winter, when snow lies white upon the memories of a lifetime, presenting new images, rare vistas, and strange symbols to the familiar eye.   This lane will share a man's happiness, and by its own beauty will make it double-dear.   In times of stress, when the private world has crumbled, and even the kindest word of dearest friend seems an impotent intrusion, this lane, by its stillness and sameness and strength, will remind a man of former times, when all was well; thereby setting his present pain in truer perspective.

To the right, as you walk, a splendid view opens over the plain, revealing the three Brickhills—Great, Little, and Bow—until at last the lane climbs a narrow stone bridge

c

THE CANAL AT SYMPSON

across the Grand Union Canal, which at this point looks more like a river than an obsolete highway of commerce, having a snug cottage perched upon the bridge's apex. Turn right, here, into the village of Sympson.

Sympson is not quite so lovely as it was in my boyhood, but it *is* lovely. Wesleyanism having broken from the simplicity of its courtly founder, is guilty here of a horrible mistake, dated in the 1930's. No doubt the mistake is centrally-heated and electrically-lighted, but two wrongs do not make a right, and the native will recall sadly the older chapel that stood when I was a child. This was a very ugly and a very crude chapel, but was far more in harmony with the simple and narrow piety of the grooms, labourers, farmers, and small shopkeepers who held the torch of Christian Liberalism above the gloom of extreme Toryism and mere Socialism. A new terrace of new houses blares newly amid the relics of a lovelier style, but against these it is not hard to close the mind's eye, so that the jagged outlines of thatch and timber and barn prevail.

The church has some good features. Its altar is dated 1632, and I recall having been present when a *piscina* was discovered behind some Erastian plaster.

Sevinstone, as it used to be called, belonged to Edith, wife of Edward the Confessor, who was the last Saxon to hold it. During the eighteenth century the manor passed to the Hanmer family, who were not, I think, important. Their memorials adhere to, but do not beautify, the walls of the church. The fine old farmhouse, a little below the inn,

SYMPSON, FROM " BLACKBERRY LANE "

has been in the Sibthorp family for several centuries; Sibthorps themselves having dwelt at Sympson since the Middle Ages, yeomen of the antique breed, whose decay it is now unfashionable to mourn.

> The forthright yeoman, master of his own,
> who yields to no man in his dignity,
> carries his brown head high, yet is discreet,
> and thinks himself demeaned if he forget
> to make a proud obeisance to the Squire.

At the cross-roads before the church, take the road sign-posted to Milton Keynes—a new wide way, mere by-pass to nowhere save a handful of remote villages. The old road (it was sacrificed twenty years ago) runs alongside, pathetically and beautifully, and at length, after a few hundred yards, gives up the hopeless race; at which point we cross a stile on the right, and follow the footpath to Caldecote.

If you are feeling so energetic that you can walk another couple of miles, or so lazy that you cannot walk *more* than another couple of miles, I strongly advise you to attempt a diversion. Instead of proceeding right, to Caldecote (as we shall presently do), take the left footpath—between wire netting—across the fields *away from* Caldecote and in the direction of a farm, half-left. Having rejoined the road, which bent widely to meet you, turn left upon it, past a trim mansion with trim stables, and follow the next lane that bears away leftward. This will carry you to Walton Church.

Walton Church stands alone in a field, within a few feet of a delightful small stream, the Lovat, just wide enough for swimming, its banks sedgy and green and cool. The church, which is dedicated to Saint Michael, is Decorated, but has a Perpendicular tower and some splendid carvings near to the *sedilia*. Behind the church, visible in winter between trees, stands Walton Hall, an agreeable country home, built

PRIOR TO
SEPTEMBER 1838
THE SOUTHERN PART
OF THIS RAILWAY
TERMINATED AT
THIS BRIDGE
WHENCE
PASSENGERS WERE
CONVEYED BY COACH
TO RUGBY WHERE
THEY REJOINED THE
RAILWAY FOR
BIRMINGHAM

INSCRIBED BY
SIR HERBERT LEON, BART.
AND LADY LEON OF
BLETCHLEY PARK, BUCKS.
BY PERMISSION OF THE
L.&N.W.RAILWAY COMPANY
AUG. 1920.

AN INTERESTING
PLAQUE ON
DENBIGH BRIDGE

THE MAIN STREET,
FENNY
STRATFORD

120 years ago, somewhat before architecture in England went out of fashion.

Walton—or, if you care to be formal, Walton-juxta-Wavendon—is not mentioned in Domesday, having, probably, been joined with Bow Brickhill or Milton Keynes, adjacent villages. The family of Pinfold—the first Sir Thomas was Chancellor of the Diocese of Peterborough—held the advowson here in the 1600's and retained it for nearly three centuries. But history here seems a vague thing, and the comings and goings of men matters of some considerable unimportance. Here are only the stream and the church and a universe of meadowland, with Bow Brickhill's fir-clumped eminence away to the left, vivid against the skyline. At Walton we may say:

> Beside this cooing stream of high summer
> I pass the day in solitary joy,
> busily idle, supine in the sun,
> stark to the glow and zenith of the noon,
> a universe alone amid the reeds.
> Above these two tall elms I see the tower
> of church beside the willow on the water,
> and—over meadows—gracious, white, and cool
> against the brazen stooks and burnished wheat,
> the manor shines in mellowness of age,
> alone, withdrawn, sequestered, tinged by time
> . . . then silence and this universe of fields,
> mile upon mile, with here and there a cottage
> carved in a dell, or rising from a wood
> naturally, like ash and oak and elm,
> born to the manner, woven with the garment.

This, I say, is a delightful place, and (if the weather is kind) yours will have been a pilgrimage of grace, from which you will return refreshed and the better able to endure the progress that slew the church and the Hall and its ancient inmates, and is getting ready to slay itself.

Caldecote is an interesting example of decay. Two

CARVED FIGURES
AND THE TOWER,
BOW BRICKHILL
CHURCH

THE LANE TO
BOW BRICKHILL
CHURCH

CROSSING THE LINE AT BOW BRICKHILL HALT

hundred years ago it was a thriving hamlet.   To-day it consists of a farm and some outbuildings.

After Caldecote, you cross the stream by a plank, and
then follow over the railway line from Bletchley to Bedford.
The path begins to climb slowly, from 200 to 600 feet,
giving some splendid views ahead, of Bow Brickhill and the
fir woods there, capped by its squat strong church.

The footpath enters the road leading to Bow Brickhill.
Turn leftward along this way, following through the hill-
side village, and thence along a sandy path to the church at
the summit.

Bow Brickhill is the smallest of the three Brickhills.   I
cannot say that it is the fairest, except when I am in it,
for at other times, when I am at Great or Little Brickhill, it
seems then that these are the fairest.   The village, at all

events, is strung along a hill, and the houses appear to grow smaller as the lane climbs higher.   The inn at the foot of the village, for instance, is—or seems to be—a very considerable building, but the last of the white cottages on the summit looks to be a toy cottage, a doll's house rather than a human habitation.   Towards the crest of the hill, indeed, where the lane sprouts into cobbles, the place becomes as it were a Cornish fishing village *sans* the sea.

The word *Bow* derives from an ancient local family that once lived here, the Boels; and *Brickhill* is taken from the peculiar reddish hue of the sandy soil, an outcrop of Bedfordshire.   The manor has belonged to many famous families—Giffards, Clares, and Staffords, Boels, Audleys, and Russells—and it was an eighteenth-century lord of this manor, Francis Hooke, who planted many thousands of fir trees in the neighbourhood and more especially upon the slopes of this village.

WALTON HOUSE

THE VIEW FROM BOW BRICKHILL

The Church of All Saints possesses many notable features, and is worth a visit.   Unfortunately its rector chooses to keep the place locked during week-days—a habit that came in, alongside much else that is obnoxious and unmannerly, with the lapse of Faith.   In the Middle Ages the churches of Christendom were not shut.   The weekday wayfarer, therefore, must content himself by a peep through the windows, and the snippet of news that this church was used as a telegraph station to France during the first world war.

Having been denied sight of the interior, he must turn instead to a sight that cannot be denied—the long sweep of landscape at his feet, as pleasant a stretch of English countryside as a man may wish to see.   To the left are Oxfordshire and Buckinghamshire, with glimpses of the Cotswolds on a clear day.   Ahead lies Northamptonshire, the County of " spires and squires "; and to the right, almost over our shoulder, is the border of Bedfordshire.

To me regarding it after many years' absence, on a morning of early spring, this view is especially poignant, for it was here, among a green and moderate landscape, that as a child I came first to know the countryside and England, learning for myself, through many a delectable walk and petty adventure, of its birds, its beasts, and its flowers; its rivers, woods, and hills; its villages and churches and folk.   I have ancestral ties with Cumberland —a gaunt land, huge, towering, bony—and with the West also—sea-sprayed and heathered and deep-delled—but here, for better and for worse, amid moderate beauties and lesser levels, I made my debut to nature, and as it were introduced my English self to England.

It is a solemn and a joyful experience to stand by the door of this church and, gazing over the land far below, to recognize the villages scattered there; to light upon a

THE CANAL NEAR STOKE HAMMOND

thatched roof or one gleaming house, and gradually by the power of the imagination to draw it nearer, so that the roof grows large and clear, and gives place to terrace and pond and lawn, and at last to the faces within the rooms, long dead, or scattered, or made mere memories by many another of Time's ungracious tricks.

At the far end of the churchyard, on its right, a small gate leads into the sandy track that brought you to the church. Join this track leftward for five yards. Here, on the right, you cross a battered fence and, after five more yards, emerge rightward on to a wide grassy path. Here at once you will see more closely what has been evident to you since first from Blackberry Lane you sighted the crest of the Bow— that this is a tract of country more akin to Surrey than to

Buckinghamshire, sandy and spread with many coniferous trees, descendants of the sires planted by a lord of the manor.

Follow this grassy track, and forge directly ahead towards a gap on the skyline—a wartime clearing—through which another splendid vista appears. Ignore, please, the gratuitous and expensively painted "Private Drive" notices. These are tasteful, it is true, but suffer from the defect of inaccuracy, since this route is neither private nor yet a drive. Villagers have walked freely along it from time immemorial, and, at least until we are all nationalized, I trust that you also will observe the ancient and honourable precedent set by your forebears. Do not be deterred even by the delicately unattractive villa that some fellow has been allowed to build on this isolated haven.

At the clearing, on the brow of the hill, you will derive

LOOKING TOWARDS QUAINTON

THE RIVER LOVAT AT WALTON

the full reward of your arduous climb from Caldecote. In front lie the plain-land villages of Wing and Stewkley and Aston Abbots, their magnificent churches gleaming in the sunlight. In the middle distance the smoke from Bletchley Junction brings silent news of the world. Far away, to the right of the picture, flat upon the plain, Whaddon and Shenley and Loughton and Bradwell, and half a hundred other hamlets, wait patiently for what the times will bring; not greatly changed since Drake sent the fire-ships into Calais, and scarcely at all changed since Nelson came on deck wearing his Orders.

At the bottom of the hill your path crosses a small brook and a grassy track, and continues onward, skirting the fir trees on its right. Early in the morning, or at night, this valley offers a vivid contrast between the natural and the urban life, between country and town, the old and the new, the obsolete and the vogue, perennial and ephemeral. On the one hand is the brook's voice, silver-trickling between sandy banks, exhilarating in gladness, and to sadness a lullaby. Here, you feel, is the peace of strength and a symphony of natural sounds, a vast silence having as *motif* the breeze and the bird song and this brook. Suddenly, and upon the other hand, comes the " still, sad music of humanity ", a rumbling lorry or the crackle of an adolescent sports-car from the Watling Street, high above, on your right. At such moments a man must make his choice— not, indeed, as to whether he shall have the one or the other entirely, for that is not possible, brooks being not ubi- quitous, and motor-cars having long ago taken firm clutch upon man's windpipe—but rather which of the two he shall accept as the more lovely, the more healthy, and the less compatible with neurosis.

At the far end of the wood you must cross a second stream, and make for a gate on the left of the next meadow.

Having crossed this meadow, look slightly rightward for a stile on the skyline, and when you have reached this, pause to sample the view behind you.   Here the wooded slopes of Bow Brickhill rise steeply towards the sky, and the wanderings of your late footpath can be seen through meadow, thicket, and woodland, till at length they creep up the hill, and topple over on the other side, out of sight.

Two minutes' walking will bring you onto the Watling Street, where you turn left into Little Brickhill.

Little Brickhill has remained surprisingly unspoiled by the tens of thousands of motor-cars and motor-lorries that pass through it during a busy twenty-four hours.   There is (inevitably nowadays) a tea-shop bearing ye olde-fashioned sign *Ye Olde Tea-Shoppe*, and its bread and butter may in fact be very old indeed, for all that I know or care ; but most of the houses are sensible, and two-thirds of them are ancient.   The pseudo-manor at the north-west end of the

THE WAY TO WILLEN

village is a modern pity, but the church, standing pro-
minent upon a mound at the other end of the main street,
contains enough features to outweigh the manor house.

The chancel of this church was repaired by Browne Willis,
the great historian of Buckinghamshire, who was himself
Lord of the Manors of Fenny Stratford, Water Eaton, and
Bletchley.   This last village he would not now recognize,
it having recently been " improved " to the well-known
architectural excellence of Golders Green, with a *pastiche* of
Wigan and outer Reading thrown in for variety's sake and
to emphasize the versatility of contemporary planners.
The *citoyen* whose sympathies lie with the Left will find
grim satisfaction from one of the memorial tablets in Little
Brickhill Church.   " Here lyeth the body of True Blue,
who departed this life January 172$\frac{2}{3}$.   Also the body of
Eleanor, wife of True Blue, who departed this life January
ye 21 172$\frac{4}{5}$ aged 59."   No one knows anything more of
these staunch scions of privilege.

In the reign of Richard I Little Brickhill was held by a
Norman baron, and passed through many hands before
coming into the Duncombe family in 1696.   This village,
like Brill and many another, is an example of a place that
once was notable and now is not so, save to the non-feudal
carmen who may or may not think well of its " Good Pull
Up ".   Between 1443 and 1638 the Assizes and General
Gaol Delivery for Buckinghamshire were held here, and
the village was in fact the first judgement seat on the
Norfolk circuit.   The gallows stood on a heath bordering
the road into Woburn, something less than half a mile from
the church.   Between 1561 and 1620 the names of forty-
two executed criminals were entered upon the parish register
here.

At the cross-roads by the church, follow the lane sign-
posted to Great Brickhill, a pleasant country road that

D

meanders and veers and goes up and falls down like a rustic scenic railway, having superb views away to its right, and chestnut palings for trim border at each side. In high summer the trees meet overhead, and in autumn the path is paved by most of the spectrum. Near to Great Brickhill the lane enters an outcrop of Bedfordshire sand and gorse, very alive in winter, and in summer wonderfully cool.

After a mile or so you come upon the village, an ancient and straggling place, with excellent church and many Tudor cottages. Various by-lanes dissect the place, and the walker may be left to sample these for himself. Each will yield a full harvest of thatch and rafter and garden.

Brickella, as it was called, belonged to Tostig, the famous Earl of Northumberland, but was bestowed by William I upon the Earl of Chester, that redoubtable lord of the northern Welsh Marches. It passed in time to several Buckinghamshire families—Boels and Bissets among them

—and in 1527 was sold to William Duncombe by Sir George Somerset, grandson of the Duke of Somerset by one of his Grace's fair companions.

During the Civil Wars, Lord Essex, General of the Parliament's army, was stationed here, and held a council of war at the village in July 1643.

The church, dedicated to the Nativity of the Blessed Virgin, is old and interesting. Unlike her sister in Bow Brickhill, the place is not locked during the week. The chancel was rebuilt by the Duncombes in 1602, and by one year is Elizabethan. A piece of land called Bell Rope Piece was formerly let at £2 10s. per annum, to buy bell-ropes and to pay the ringers.

With Great Brickhill we come to the last of this trio of delightful place-names—typical English place-names that are merged for ever with the traditions of English music, worthy of Purcell and Delius, and not scorned by Elgar and Warlock and Vaughan Williams.

> Claydons (Middle, East, and Steeple)
> Summer Heath and Speen,
> Brickhills (Bow and Great and Little)
> Lee and Lacey Green.

At the centre of the village, hard by the inn, is a sign-post at the cross-roads. Follow the lane towards Heath-and-Reach, which is a hamlet across the border into Bedford-shire, but strike a track running to the right after a few yards. This track soon bisects itself into two footpaths. Take the one to the right, across a sloping meadow and thence into the seclusion of the south-westerly tip of King's Wood, a massive plantation set with firs and some larch, the latter graciously slim and dappled in early May. No birds sing here, for the leaves impede sunlight, but the silence is welcome, and the soft tread of feet upon bracken

GREAT LINFORD, THE CHURCH AND ALMSHOUSES

and grass and fallen cones is itself a delectable absence of sound.

Along this footpath you may surrender yourself to half an hour of slow ambling through silent woodland and amid bracken that changes colour and texture with the season, so that summer lacks what winter owns, and winter does not vie with summer. This wood is always cool, and wintry only beneath snow. The path is indeed a joy to tread. It puts me in mind of that passage in Stevenson's book describing a night among the pines, and his lordly scattering of coin upon the pathway.

For a part of the way you are in Bedfordshire, with the pleasant market town of Leighton Buzzard a mile or more to the south-east, and the scattered hamlet of Heath-and-Reach due east.

As the way comes upon a clearing, the roof of an ancient farmhouse can be seen over the brow of the hill, a few hundred yards to the right. Very soon the path veers away in that direction, to join the by-lane leading from the skyline. Do not follow that way, but bear slightly leftward, along the smaller path; and this, after 300 yards, turns right, over a stile, and enters the lane that has been bearing down upon you from the right, exactly opposite to the Bedfordshire–Buckinghamshire border sign.

Having taken this lane, turn sharp left along it. The way climbs sharply and descends steeply through fir trees, until, after perhaps a quarter of a mile, it juts upwards to meet the highway between Woburn and Leighton Buzzard.

Motor-buses will take you thence into the main-line station at Leighton, which is forty miles from London, or into Aylesbury.

CHAPTER THREE

FROM NEWPORT PAGNELL, THROUGH MOULSOE, MILTON
  KEYNES, AND THE TWO WOOLSTONES, TO WILLEN AND
  GREAT LINFORD. (ABOUT 14 MILES)

NEWPORT PAGNELL, which stands fourteen miles from the
county town of Buckingham, on the fringe of the Northamptonshire border, being served by a railway and some motor-
buses, is an historic and comely country town of great
antiquity, whose foundations were laid by the Romans,
who, according to one school of antiquaries, named the
district *Lactodorum*.   Newport flourished after the Romans
had left Britain.

   In the reign of Edward the Confessor the manor of
Newport, whose second name had not then been bestowed
upon it, belonged to Ulf, a thane, and was granted by
William I to Fitz-Ausculf, Lord of Dudley and of eighty-six
other manors.   Even in the Middle Ages the town had its
own burgesses, and Bury Field, as it is now called, marked
the area in which they dwelt.   The word *port*, incidentally,
did not in Saxon times mean a *harbour* only; a Saxon *port*
might well be an inland *town* or *market-place*.   No doubt
the present Port Field has associations with the Roman Port
Way.

   During the reign of William Rufus the lordship of Newport passed (either by ordinance or through inheritance, it
is not known how) to Sir Fulk Paganell, Baron of Dudley,
the son of a Norman nobleman.   This Sir Fulk founded
the adjacent priory of Tickford.   His son, Ralph, fought
with Queen Maud against King Stephen.

   After many changes the town came into the possession
of Richard Neville, Earl of Warwick, on whose death at

Barnet Field it became the property of the Duke of Clarence. In 1577 it was granted by Edward VI to the Princess Elizabeth, and after her death, in 1603, it became a part of the dowry of James I's wife. Charles I sold Newport Pagnell to Sir Francis Annesley, Bt., whose descendants were created Earls of Anglesea and Barons of Newport Pagnell; the latter title became extinct, after litigation over a disputed legitimacy.

In Newport Pagnell is Dungeon Lane, near to the site of an ancient castle.

The church, standing back a little from the main street, at the north-east of the town, was built by the medieval priors of Tickford, and has been restored too thoroughly.

To-day this historic market town is historic still; nor have Messrs. Woolworth and our comrades of the " Co-op." been able to dim its charm, although the bitter blend of pink-and-green shop-fronts makes one suspect that the inability was not due to a lack of effort. There are some blemishes here, of course, and the eastern environs of the town, with their puce cut-price-palaces, appear to have undergone an acute attack of prosperity towards the end of the last century. Yet, on the whole, Newport Pagnell is well able to hold its own among the small market towns of the Midlands.

For many hundreds of years this place was the centre of the English lace industry. For several centuries lace was made by hand, and in any guide-book of the last century you will find some entry such as this, for most of the villages here: " The females of the place are engaged in lace making ". In 1768, however, a person in Nottingham, having nothing better to do, invented a machine for making lace cheaply and swiftly. The craft soon afterwards waned, and, by a supreme irony, the term " real " lace (coined by the machinists themselves) is applied nowadays only to hand-

ON THE GRAND JUNCTION CANAL

SUMMER-TIME IN NORTH BUCKINGHAMSHIRE

made lace; the rest, it seems, being not real lace. People who now desire to buy " real " lace must find one of the few craftswomen hereabouts who still have that knack. Such old women, who were to be found in these villages, even during my boyhood, must think it strange that a skill which in their own youth was common enough and poorly paid, is to-day much sought-after, and well rewarded, and regarded with vulgar awe. Many thousands of English men and women now pass drab lives tending machines that make lace; but " real " lace is made only by a handful of old women in Buckinghamshire, or by a small band of experts who find it profitable to go against the times for the benefit of that tiny minority among us who still delight in what is good. I suppose that the voice of

Mr. H. J. Massingham is one crying in the wilderness to-day; but future ages, if any such survive the wonders of science, may well recognize him for the true prophet, as to-day Carlyle is recognized for true prophet, and Ruskin, and Morris, and the poet Edward Thomas, all of whom delighted in things English that were seemly and honest, and hated the whirr of a machinery that is as false and facile as the precision of Euclid's geometry.

From Newport Pagnell the way lies along the Woburn road, leaving the site of the ancient Priory on the left, and taking the first lane on that side, signposted to North Crawley.   After a few hundred yards, and just this side of Tickford Farm, you must strike a track, away to the right, which soon afterwards becomes a footpath, and enters Moulsoe, having crossed a tributary of the Ouse in order to get there.

THE SIXTEENTH-CENTURY INN AT MILTON KEYNES

THE OUSE AT
NEWPORT
PAGNELL

" CHURCH
AND
STATE ",
NEWPORT
PAGNELL

Moulsoe is a delightfully sleepy hamlet, perched on the brow of a hill among plains.   William I gave the manor to Walter Giffard, Earl of Buckingham, whence it passed through many noble families—Talbots, Cowdrays, and Comptons—until, in the eighteenth century, it became the property of the Earls of Carrington.

From the locked door of the church you have two magnificent views.   To your right, beyond North Crawley, you overlook the fertile valley of the Ouse, with Moulsoe Old Wood beyond your shoulder; to your left, the whole plain of north Buckinghamshire and of southern Northamptonshire is laid flat to view, melting into Oxfordshire on the west, and merging, too, with Warwickshire and the innumerable drowsy villages cupped within the trees and the hills, and girt about by blue small streams.

As Gerard Manley Hopkins saw it:

> Landscape plotted and pieced—fold, fallow, and plough;
> And all trades, their gear and tackle and trim.

From Moulsoe (whose name is pronounced Mulso) you follow the winding lane westward for half a mile, until it joins the Newport Pagnell road once more, where you turn left and continue through Broughton, which is not full of beauty.   In Broughton you turn rightward along a lane into Milton Keynes, as fine a small English village as you are likely to encounter in these parts, or, for that matter, in any other parts.

Milton Keynes is a homely place.   Fields encroach upon the dusty by-lane, and brim over the scattered cottages. There is nothing here of the conventional beauty spot, for indeed no one seems to have heard of the place, save the handful of its inhabitants; and these think so well of it that they rarely leave it, and then only upon compulsion, like Falstaff.   I have known and loved Milton Keynes since

I was a boy, but at no time in my legion pilgrimages thither have I met a stranger. It takes longer to travel from London to Milton Keynes than it does to travel from London to Bath—a fact for which some men will be profoundly thankful.

Whenever I pass this way I am reminded of the innumerable personal associations that hover in the spirit of places; and I recall the lines:

> Scattered up and down the land
> quiet, sequestered places stand:
> places where I stopped to stare:
> places where I watched the hare:
> places steeped in summer sun
> where I heard the river run
> with a murmur through the meadows
> as I listened in the shadows.

Edith, Queen to Edward the Confessor, held a part of the lands here. At the beginning of the reign of Henry II, Anabell, heiress of the Peverills, who then were lords of the

ENTERING MOULSOE

place, married Hugh de Cahines, or Keynes, whose surname was given to Milton. It was a William de Keynes who captured King Stephen at the battle of Lincoln, but the King refusing to make formal surrender to a commoner, the Earl of Gloucester was summoned, to whom Stephen yielded his sword. The manor was granted by Henry VII to Sir Edward Poynings, who did such sound work in the old English tradition of trying to stop the Irish from slaughtering one another. Staffords were the next lords; they held the manor for nearly 300 years, when it passed to the Earl of Winchelsea and Nottingham.

The church at Milton Keynes, which is among the finest in the Kingdom, and is a perfect instance of a parish church in the Decorated style, is approached through a line of small trees, having a farm that reaches to the church wall itself, so that cows sometimes browse upon the backs of unsuspecting worshippers who have stopped to discuss the result of the Crimean War, or whatever else passes for news in this most blessed haven of pristine sanity.

At the inn you will strike a footpath south-west to Woughton-on-the-Green. On your left, as you walk, you will see the fir-clad slopes of Bow Brickhill and—ahead— the high ground of Bradwell and Calverton, 400 feet above the sea. Just before it enters Woughton, this path crosses the Ouse. Here primroses abound beneath oaks in early spring, and snowdrops about the elms and in hedgerows. Fritillaries, too, have been found in this district; but I was never much of a botanist, and am content to love a flower, as deeply as I can love most objects, without hankering after the precise name by which (according to English botanists) the imperial Romans would have called it, had they ever encountered it. *Clematis Vitalba* sounds well, but I prefer *Old Man's Beard.*

Woughton-on-the-Green is a small hamlet with a good

inn, some fine cottages, and a spruce manor standing back a little from the lane.   At the time of the Conquest, *Vlchetone*, as it was then called, belonged to the Earls of Morton, from whom it passed, through many hands, to the Verleys, Muxons, Greys, Vavasours, and Mordaunts.

You will not, I think, feel alarmed that the rest of this walk lies along the road, for a part of the way is little more than a track, and in any event you will have to travel a great distance indeed before you discover a lovelier stretch of winding English lane.

As you walk you may say with the poet:

> I too love roads:
> the high-banked bend that goads
> the curious mind:
> looking back at twined
> crossways: and
> the weatherbeaten hand
> of signpost
> nudging at the lost
> traveller,
> whispering to him, " Sir,
> follow me
> and presently you'll see
> —well, follow me
> and see what you shall see."

Pass through Woughton-on-the-Green, bearing slightly rightward, towards a trio of delightful hamlets, each " a one-eyed, blinking sort of place ", Great Woolstone, Little Woolstone, and Willen.

It is not much above two miles from Woughton to Willen, and the way is at all seasons delightful.   In winter the bare elms and oaks allow glimpses of the higher ground leftward—typical north Buckinghamshire landscape of quiet fields, mile upon mile of them, studded with hedgerows, and watered by meandering streams.

The lane is sandwiched between water, for on its left,

MILTON KEYNES
CHURCH, THE
NAVE

MILTON KEYNES
CHURCH, THE
EXTERIOR

TUDOR COTTAGES
AT MILTON
KEYNES

CROSS-ROADS,
MILTON KEYNES

above the level of the road, the canal runs (or, rather, dawdles), and is more like a river than a conventional canal, being spanned here and there by mellow grey bridges, and having sundry snug cottages engulfed upon its banks, and several footpaths loitering casually to and from the main-land.   On your right the slow stream meanders, sometimes to within a few yards of the lane—a boon to small boys in high summer, and to males of all ages who, having nothing better to do, do what is best by taking a rod and dipping it hopefully into the dimpled water, not over-zealous about the fish, but very intent indeed upon the sun and the flowers and the leaves' green shade against the stream. From time to time you will find—if your luck happens to be in that morning—men whose speech you can scarcely fathom, rich racy lords of furrow and scythe; and women with bright shawls and tanned faces, far too worldly-wise ever to become merely pretty; and gypsy girls that seem a very sound argument against marriage, unless indeed they are an argument in its favour.

Great Woolstone, or *Vlieston* as it was called at the time of Domesday, was held, under Walter Giffard, of the foreign monks of Saint Peter de Culture, and is now in the possession of the Selby-Lowndes, one of the oldest families in the Kingdom, lords also of Whaddon, away to the south-west.

" The Barge Inn ", along this lane, bears testimony to the hey-day of canal transport.   I suppose that I have entered this place not less than fifty times, yet I have never seen a man there who did not carry a scythe, or wear leggings, or smoke a clay pipe, or talk of London as though it were a distant phantom thousands of miles away upon a faint horizon.

Little Woolstone has an unexpected claim to fame, for it was a Woolstone man, one Smith, who invented and (wisely) patented the once-famous steam cultivator that ousted ox and horse, and was itself dethroned by the infernal combustion engine. In 1861 Mr. Smith's steam cultivator ploughed up a crop of coins bearing as motto the words *Regus et Regulus.*

At Willen there is a notable church and a fine vicarage, but upon weekdays, alas, the parson chooses to keep the former building closed. The technical term for the style of Willen Church is Debased Gothic, but that gives a false impression, and in no way does justice to the Wren-like appearance of the place—Wren-like, because the great man himself is said to have sketched the outlines of the plan. Willen Church was built by Dr. Busby, that famous Master of Westminster School who declined to doff his hat in the presence of the Sovereign because, he said, to do so would diminish his own dignity in the eyes of the boys. Dr. Busby, at all events, inherited the manor of Willen, by Act of Parliament, from the three daughters of Colonel Hammond, who held personal custody of Charles I at Carisbrooke Castle. He stipulated that the incumbent should always be a former Westminster Student of Christchurch. Not the least pleasing feature of Willen is its avenue of fine elms, leading from the vicarage to the church.

Willen is unspoiled because it is unknown. The cottages here wear an air of permanence; the oaks have a great girth; and old men are hale. A touch of the bizarre comes from the raised footpaths that lead out of the hamlet—raised against the vagaries of the river Ouse, which often floods during autumn and early spring.

From Willen take the by-lane to Great Linford, leaving a small covert to your right, and climbing slowly until, at Grange Farm, you stand 300 feet above the sea. Thereafter the way crosses a stream. A mile and a half of pleasant, gentle going awaits you before this lane crosses

ENTERING NEWPORT PAGNELL

the canal and bears right into Great Linford.   Great Linford is an inland port, not so prosperous now as during last century, when the canal trade was at its zenith, but evidently a place of some importance still, and an attractive village in its own right.

It is worth while to spend a little time on the quay, where you will find a good inn alongside the jetty, and some business-like mooring rings.   A land-bound mariner will feel at home here, the more especially because sundry gentlemen in peaked caps and blue sweaters lounge against the quayside and, amid puffs from clay pipes, gaze wistfully across the water—several yards of it—to the green bank opposite.   From time to time a barge will draw

BARGES APPROACHING GREAT LINFORD

alongside, and her motley crew will leap ashore—father and son in trim caps, to be about their mariners' business; mother, very bronzed and shawled and crisp-tongued; and some children without shoes but with a very healthy glow upon their faces.

If you are fortunate the barge will not be motor-driven, but will have instead a plodding horse for motive power, pleasantly bejangled and brassy about the mane, massively strong and inhumanly patient, gathering depth, as it seems, from the blinkered narrowness of his vision, and manifestly having wise things to utter, had he but the gift of speech.

If you care to ask the captain, you may even enjoy the experience of going on board, and then of examining the snug quarters below decks—marvellously clean, as clean as a Dutch merchantman, glowing with bright brass and speckless glass and dazzling paintwork, everything ship-shape-and-Bristol-fashion, neat enough to delight a Pay-master Commander.

In 1066 there were two manors in *Linforde*, each held by Hugh de Bolebec, one of the tenant-in-chief, Walter Giffard, the other of the Crown.   These two manors passed to Hugh's son, who founded the Abbey of Woburn in 1145, and thence to many families—the Earls of Ormonde, the Saint Legers, Princess Elizabeth, Richard Campion.   The ancient family of Andrewes of Lathbury were at one time lords of the manor of Great Linford.

The Church of Saint Andrew has many fine features in the Early Decorated style, but was painfully restored during the last century, when most of the tracery in the windows was spoiled, and the ceilings covered by an unlovely plaster.

At the eastern end of the churchyard are some quaint grey-stone buildings, each designed to contain seven tene-ments, one being three storeys high and the others one

BRITISH RAILWAYS, GREAT LINFORD

storey.   These buildings were erected by a former lord of
the manor, Sir William Pritchard, as almshouses for six of
the village poor, the centre home being reserved for a school
and its teacher.

In the past, before charity came to be nationalized, various
picturesque charities were bestowed upon Great Linford
by its local gentry.   One pound sterling was given to the
rector, upon condition that he did not allow any beasts to
graze in the churchyard; and the same sum was awarded
to the parish clerk, for keeping the pews and windows
clean.   Six times that amount was given at Christmastime,
to be spent upon breeches and a gown for six almsmen, and
upon a gown and petticoat for six almswomen.

Your sojourn at Great Linford may be prolonged to
coincide with the arrival (and subsequently the departure)
of the single line railway into Newport Pagnell.

CHAPTER FOUR

FROM BUCKINGHAM TO STOWE, LILLINGSTONE DAYRELL,
AND BACK INTO CHACKMORE. (ABOUT 10 MILES)

BUCKINGHAM, the county town, is served by a branch railway and by motor-buses that radiate into Bicester and
beyond the border of Northamptonshire; and because
Buckingham and Stowe are places of very great historical
interest, this chapter will appeal especially to the reader
who would rather saunter and see than march and meditate.

Buckingham is famous—that is, if it *is* famous—for its
Duchy, with which, indeed, it has been closely linked
throughout its long and chequered history. The town
has some Saxon associations, and several antiquaries believe
that at Thornborough Bridge, not far out of the town,
was fought the great battle between Claudius's general,
Aulus Plautius, and the sons of King Cymbeline, A.D. 44.

In A.D. 806 King Alfred divided his realm into shires, and
Buckingham was then selected to be the capital of the
County. The *Anglo-Saxon Chronicle* relates that in A.D. 918
Edward the Elder raised an army at Bernwood in order to
repel a Danish inroad from the Fens and Northamptonshire. Edward built two forts at Buckingham, athwart the
river there.

Queen Elizabeth paid the town a State visit in 1568; and
during the Civil Wars the place stood staunchly for the
King, but was overrun after the fall of Hillesden House,
the Royalist stronghold nearby. It was from Buckingham
that Charles I learned of the birth of Princess Henrietta in
Exeter, whither her mother had fled from the Roundheads.

In 1725 a great part of the old town was destroyed by fire,

A SIXTEENTH-CENTURY FARMHOUSE NEAR BUCKINGHAM

and Buckingham as a centre of trade never recovered from the shock. Neglected by main lines, set in the core of a farming world, flanked by other farming counties—Oxfordshire, Northamptonshire, and Bedfordshire—Buckingham fell back in the race for an industrial revolution. To-day—save for a small suburb of typically modern, and therefore utterly despicable, pink villas—Buckingham is a small country town, scarcely larger than a large village, a place of some quietness of soul.

The Duchy of Buckingham (it is now extinct, and will probably not be revived) had a most intricate career, full of history and adventure, and not without genealogical interest also. Humphrey Plantagenet, great-grandson of Thomas of Woodstock, a son of Henry III, was created first Duke of Buckingham by Henry VI in 1445, with a special grant (to himself and his heirs) of precedence over all English and Norman Dukes, save only those of the Blood. In the sixteenth century the Duchy became extinct, but was revived by James I in the person of his popinjay favourite, the son of Sir George Villiers, whom he created Earl (1616), Marquis (1617), and at last Duke (1623) of Buckingham— an escapade, I believe, without parallel in the annals of the English peerage. The Duke's son, having served the King faithfully throughout the Rebellion, died in disgraceful poverty, and for a second time the title lapsed.

Fifteen years later the Duchy was revived in John Sheffield, Earl of Mulgrave, who was created Duke of Buckingham and Normanby.

Once more the title lapsed; but in 1822 the son of the Marquis of Buckingham, Richard Grenville Nugent Chandos Temple, became, by letters patent, Duke of Buckingham and Chandos. The name of this family was afterwards elongated to become Plantagenet-Temple-Nugent-Brydges-Chandos-Grenville, for what purpose is uncertain. The mother of the penultimate Duke was sole descendant of Mary, Queen of France, herself a sister of Henry VIII; and if that King's will had been observed after his death, the Duke of Buckingham and Chandos might have become King of England.

Although many of its medieval features have disappeared, Buckingham retains several ancient landmarks; in Market Hill, for example, stood Christ's Hospital, founded by Queen Elizabeth in 1597, rather as a refuge for the poor and the aged than as a medical asylum; and some vestiges remain of the chantry chapel of the Buckingham Guild of Holy Trinity.

Two men who were connected with Buckingham seem

THE VALE OF AYLESBURY, FROM KOP HILL

worthy of mention. The first, Browne Willis, sat in the House of Commons as a member for the Borough from 1705 until 1709. So great was his gratitude for this honour that thereafter he never mentioned the name of the town without adding that it was " the county town ". Browne Willis persuaded the Bishop of Lincoln (within whose diocese Buckingham lay) and the Archdeacon to hold their visitations in the town; and the church was well repaired at his own expense. Browne Willis was in some respects the most remarkable figure in County history. Certainly few Buckinghamshire men have been more zealous in their love of the County. He was Rector of Bletchley and Lord of the Manor there, having built for himself a house in Water Eaton, formerly a picturesque hamlet a mile from the village, with a mill and a stream that were pleasant to fishermen and small boys and young lovers. His history of the County is now, of course, out of date, and upon points of scholarship also it has been superseded; but the work remains essential to a full understanding of Buckinghamshire before the Industrial Revolution.

The second Buckingham worthy was Robert Hill, who became known as the learned tailor of Buckingham. This remarkable person, who anticipated many of Smiles' self-helps, was born at Miswell, near Tring, in the adjacent county of Hertfordshire, and was apprenticed, when fourteen years old, to his stepfather, a tailor and maker of stays in the town. He taught himself to read and write, and having procured an English dictionary and a Latin Grammar, spent his leisure moments—they must have been few—in studying the two languages. Having disposed of the Romans, the sturdy apprentice took upon himself to conquer the Greeks, a battle that lasted (as we are told) throughout three years, at the end of which time he had vanquished that elusive race and also (one presumes) the

THE CORINTHIAN
ARCH, STOWE

MAY DAY IN
STOWE PARK

vagaries of *oida*. Being no longer *in statu pupillarii*, he set up as schoolmaster, but early got into difficulties, for although one of his scholars could explain the conduct of decimal fractions, he himself had not progressed beyond the vexations of common long division. Here, one regrets to say, the master cheated, for in order to allow himself enough time in which to overhaul the pupil, he ordered that unhappy and too-learned youth to copy out the tables of decimal fractions in Wingate's Arithmetic, a task that took six weeks. After this bout the tailor took to his bed—that least noxious of the many other things to which he might have resorted. Nevertheless, his zeal for knowledge remained unabated, and upon meeting with some itinerant Jews, he determined to learn Hebrew. This tongue also went the way of Rome and Greece; and we are told by the late Mr. Sheahan, who seems to have known many things about Buckinghamshire, that the learned tailor was able to put the Bishop of Clogher aright on a point of Hebrew syntax.

Other worthies, however, and other places await our attention: and the first of these is Stowe and the Temple family. Stowe lies near to Buckingham, and is approached by way of the Brackley road. Follow this road out of the town for about 200 yards and turn right at the first sign-post, pointing toward Chackmore and Stowe. If you are given to meditation, the next 100 yards will afford you material to spare, for the approach to Stowe House—the avenue itself is symbolic of grace and power and the awareness of beauty—is flanked by as mean a specimen of contemporary domestic architecture as I have seen for a long while, well up to the standard of the Kingston by-pass. I have no motive in citing these particular houses. I choose them because they are typical and because their setting makes the moral of them poignantly vivid. I should be sorry indeed to know that the matter has become tedious; but the truth is, I love my country not less than you do, and I believe that some good purpose may be served, no matter how slightly or obliquely, by speaking out against these bad things.

In front of you, meanwhile, welcome like jam after bitter pill, Stowe avenue stretches as straight as a Roman road, green-verged and lined by a double row of stately elms; at whose far end, hidden first by the brow of a hill, stands the Corinthian Arch, which in turn gives way to a noble vista toward the house and the grounds.

Now, these grounds are so vast, their monuments so numerous, and the house itself so steeped in history, that a brief survey, such as this, can merely hint the broad outline of the story, leaving the reader to supplement it by reference to any of the numerous handbooks about Stowe.

Stowe—the *station*, or settlement, of Anglo-Saxon times —is first recorded in 1129. In 1600 the estates came into the Temple family (Sir Thomas Temple, whose grandfather, Sir Peter, was descended from Leofric, Earl of Leicester, having been created Baronet at that time). Thomas married into another Buckinghamshire family, the Latimers (whose country lay in the valley of the Chess), having as issue three children, whose mother lived to see four generations of her descendants, 700 of them.

Thomas Temple's grandson, Sir Robert Temple, built Stowe House, and Robert's son, afterwards Viscount Cobham, added many features to the place. Theirs were the days of Tory and Whig oligarchy, when the gentlemen of England, sometimes for good, sometimes for ill, ruled England. Theirs were the days of hospitality on a lavish scale; days of the graces and subtleties of living, when some of the poor existed in a manner that would to-day be considered unfit for beasts, and when some of the nobility

A QUIET CORNER OF
BUCKINGHAM

IN THE WOODS
NEAR GREAT
BRICKHILL

existed in a manner that is now beyond the scope or *flair* of any man at all.

To Stowe came most of the eminent statesmen, warriors, and artists of the day, to be entertained in a manner consonant with that station of life into which it had pleased God to place them. Pope has sketched such a scene in *Moral Essays*; and Thomson (of the too-tardy *Seasons*) speaks of—

the fair majestic paradise of Stowe.

This " paradise " can be seen more nearly if you will follow the footpath to the right of the Corinthian Arch, whereby you enter into the grounds, near one of two ornamental summer-houses, a vantage-point from which you may enjoy a splendid view of the lake and of the grounds sloping away to the rear of the house, a *façade* that is more impressive, I think, than the formal frontage. Bear in mind that Stowe is now a public school, and that its grounds are not public property.

Here, with the house in front of your eyes, you may care to read a little more of its story. Stowe's great days came under the Dukes of Buckingham and Chandos, and all nice people, whether they be for or against the peerage, will relish that Duke who upon hearing that his heir had accepted chairmanship of the new Great Western Railway Company, observed: " To think that a son of mine should become clerk in a railway booking office."

The last Duke's daughter was succeeded at Stowe by the Comte de Paris, but in 1918 the word *Ichabod* became more than mere writing on a wall, and the place was sold for a school that to-day ranks high and is said to have spiritual affinities with Eton. Myself, I find its traditions too slight to be impressive—a point, as I am well aware, that can have no direct bearing upon the excellences of the education offered by this very fine school. When, however,

a small boy of eleven years old is sent (as I was sent) to a school whose Houses are named after such Old Boys as Edmund Spenser, poet of *The Faerie Queen*, and Lord Clive; when, that is to say, he grows in daily contact with traditions that were four centuries old before his birth, and when, moreover, he quotes school jargon of pre-Shakespearean days—then, I suggest, he will come to gauge other schools by the yardstick of age, and will begin to inquire whatever use a school can be that is three and a half centuries younger than his own? This is a lamentable state of mind, and very delightful.

The prime difference between the ancient and the modern school is well illustrated by one small custom: whereas in the Lower Second we used upon occasions to say " *Licetne mihi exire* " Stowe boys say " May I go to Egypt ? "— the w.c.'s being near to the Egyptian entrance.   I cannot take kindly to their habit of answering " *Sto* " at roll-call. Newcome, I am certain, would have winced at this blend of theory with practice.   It is, moreover, late Latin; very late Latin; too late.   Stowe, for all that, is a first-rate public school, with a notable record and a most enviable environment.

Frankly, you are at liberty, in this chapter, to ignore my directions and to wander as you please, provided always that you observe the elementary rights of another man's garden, and keep to the defined pathways.   You will find a great deal to look at and something to admire; though perhaps, like myself, you will not be dazzled by the numerous monuments to the deceased (and, no doubt, amiable) nonentities of the Temple family.   Some of these monuments are falling into decay, unlike Horace's :

Exegi monumentum aere perennius.

If, on the other hand, you prefer to abide by these directions you will turn sharp right at the summer-house, along the path that leaves a ruined temple on its right and bears leftward, over a bridge, to the summit of a small hill.

From this summit you will see many monuments which, like Sam Weller's knowledge of London, are peculiar and extensive; so peculiar, indeed, and so extensive, that I shall not attempt to describe all of them.   Having crossed the school golf-course, you should bear slightly to the right, making for the round apex of the Bourbon tower, just visible above the leaves of a copse.   This extraordinary building was erected by the Duke to commemorate the restoration of Louis XVIII of France, who had passed much of his exile at Hartwell House, not far from Aylesbury.   The

King himself officiated at the ceremony, but the occasion cannot have been impressive, since His Majesty was too fat to walk across the grounds and had to be driven there in a carriage.

From the Bourbon Tower, looking ahead, but slightly to the right, you will see a line of trees, perhaps a quarter of a mile away, and behind them the roadway. Make towards this road—cutting across two fields in order to reach it—and then turn left along it, into the village of Lillingstone Dayrell.

Here you have twenty minutes' agreeable walking through a woodland lane that dips and rises and bends and veers, and trips across a small stream or two, and passes a house, and ignores several inviting paths that lead into the heart of the woods.

This lane will bring you on to the Northampton road, in the centre of Lillingstone Dayrell, with the church directly ahead, on the other side of the road, and a most interesting inn on the left. The inn is interesting because it appears to be a private house standing alone on a remote grassy track. Indeed, when first I saw it, and the inn sign outside it, I took the latter to be a joke. If you need refreshment, you must walk up the garden path, and turn into the back of the house, where there is a small courtyard. The inn parlour is also the inn kitchen; and the student of character will learn a great deal by spending a winter's evening there.

Lelinchestone was among the lands held by Walter Giffard at the Norman Conquest. In the thirteenth century the manor passed into the ancient family of De Hayrell, or Dayrell; and one antiquary writing seventy years ago was able to say that the same family still held land there, its lord being at that time Edmund Francis Dayrell, thirty-fourth male descendant of Elias Dairel, who was Lord of the Manor in

APRIL IN A BUCKINGHAMSHIRE BEECHWOOD

1195. Several members of this family have been High Sheriffs of the County; many more have represented Buckinghamshire in Parliament; and five have been rectors of the parish.

The original manor house was pulled down in 1767, but the present seat was built upon the site by Richard Dayrell in 1792, and is a good example of the architecture of that period.

The Church of Saint Nicholas is full of interest, having clerestory windows, intricate *piscina*, and some splendid brasses of mediæval Dayrells.

Lillingstone Dayrell is so drowsy that a man may be forgiven if he wonders whether it ever wakes. I once spent a whole hour there, lying in the grass beside the inn, watching for signs of life; and I saw none. Not so much as a solitary cur came out to bask on the summer cobbles: no carter, no cowman, no pretty girl out to see whether the men were admiring her. On the highroad one motor rumbled by, into Northampton, then a deep stillness fell upon the village. I remembered Lillingstone like that, when I was a boy. There is life here of course. Lads go forth into the world, and thrive or fail as maybe. Some women have committed adultery in this quiet place. Children have been born here and (in times past) have seen no faces but Lillingstone faces, no lanes nor hills nor fields than Lillingstone's, and in Lillingstone earth they are laid to rest. There have been robberies at Lillingstone, and violence and fraud and gay dances and elopement. And, no doubt, families have sat—may even now be sitting—around the fire, hating one another. But you would scarcely believe so—not, at all events, if you came hither (as last I came) upon a hot June forenoon, and saw only the cottages and the church and the meadows, and one wasp droning.

In a timbered cottage not far from this village lived an

old woman who could make lace—a craft, as we have seen, that is one of the glories of Buckinghamshire folk and linked with their names.   The origins of this cottage craft lie in the sixteenth century, when King Philip II of Spain so persecuted the Hugenot lacemakers of the Low Countries that they fled into England for asylum.   King Louis XIV

BOBBINS FOR LACE-MAKING

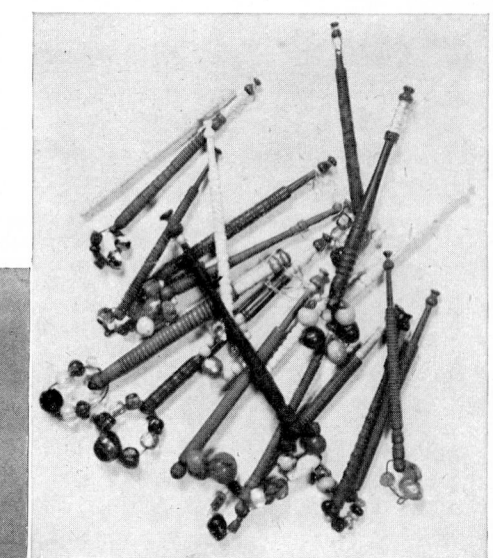

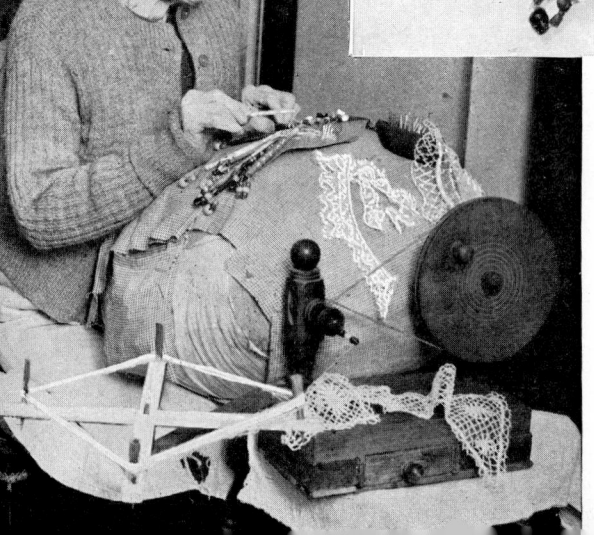

A LACE-MAKER, WHO LEARNED THE CRAFT WHEN SHE WAS 4 YEARS OLD

afterwards made the same blunder; and one of his financial ministers, the Swiss Necker, deplored His Most Catholic Majesty's treatment of these most Protestant craftsmen who, as he explained, were a source of great wealth wherever they went. Many of these Flemish refugees settled at a village not far from Lillingstone Dayrell, the small neat village of Cranfield, across the Bedfordshire border. These good people did not observe a closed-shop policy, for they lived in an age when crafts and guilds were concerned rather with the workmen's skill than with the workmen's profit-motive. They passed on their skill, so that it permeated the Kingdom, having notable centres at Honiton in Devonshire, and at Ripon in Yorkshire.

Throughout the eighteenth and nineteenth centuries the women were to be seen at their cottage doors, upon mild days, making lace. Children learned the craft before they could spell. I watched one old woman at work, several times, and her skill amazed me. Perhaps the most intricate part of the process is the design itself, which must be drawn, or traced, onto a sheet of clean white cardboard of a special texture, and afterwards pricked upon a brown board. This particular old woman, whose eyes had lost a little of their keenness (for she was eighty-five when last I saw her), used then to trace over her design with an indelible pencil, to emphasize its outlines. Next she would wind her linen threads about the bobbins, and afterwards sew her design on to a special pillow. This pillow was filled with straw, and the bobbins were then draped around it, hanging downward from the centre. If the weather was mild the old woman sat in the porch, upon a stool two feet from the ground, with her work laid in front of her. The cobbles outside the door were clearly indented by similar stools of her ancestors.

From Lillingstone Dayrell you may, if you wish, take the

motor-bus into Buckingham, or to the main-line railway at Northampton. Equally you may care to walk back into Buckingham by a slightly varied route; if you do so wish, take the footpath leftward over a small brook to the left of the inn, and thence onto the lane that you joined from Stowe.

Thereafter, I suggest that you make for the Bourbon Tower, leaving it on your left, and join the well-defined roadway running south-east towards the house. This track will take you past the front of Stowe House—a front, as I have suggested, that is less imposing than the back. Nevertheless, the house and the grounds are most impressive, and a worthy monument to what was most attractive in the eighteenth century.

A little way beyond the house you will see the two lodge gates. By the left-handed of these a pathway dips into the valley and enters a small tract of woodland, after which it veers leftward again and brings you upon the Corinthian arch.

At the arch you may either return into Buckingham as you came, down the avenue, or take the lane left into the hamlet of Chackmore (or Chalkmore), an attractive place with some fine old cottages (one of them dated 1693) and a massive elm-tree in the centre of the one street. Also of interest is the row of old cottages on the left, one of which is the inn—the only semi-detached public-house in the neighbourhood.

Just beyond this inn, on the right-hand side of the lane, a footpath strikes across three meadows, leaving the avenue away to the right, and at length climbs a hill. Directly in front—although somewhat hard to find from a distance—is a way on to the road.

Turn left on joining this road, and after a couple of hundred yards you will be back once more in the centre of Buckingham.

CHAPTER FIVE

FROM GAWCOTT AND PRESTON BISSETT TO HILLESDEN
AND THE THREE CLAYDONS. (ABOUT 13 MILES)

IT does not greatly matter at what time of year or in what
weather a man goes walking, since all seasons and every
prospect are both inevitable and timely. On a May
morning at sunrise, before even the labourers are abroad,
when a man goes into the fields, and smells the grass and
hears the blackbird or perhaps a cuckoo, he will feel that
summer is the fairest season; but equally, if he is in harmony
with life and life's reality, he will feel that the same scene,
towards nightfall in November, bleak and trim and spare
beneath vivid moon, is likewise delectable. He will at the
same time find himself in accord with even the freaks of
climate—with May's blizzard or the muggy drizzle of July—
since these whet his desire for the true season. If, moreover, he is a countryman, this concord and these delights
will be increased, for he will know then how best to mark
the seasons' waxing and waning. In December he will see
summer roses still in bloom; in July he will watch the
blackberry forming its greyish-white fruit.

Such were my thoughts as I walked from Buckingham
through Preston Bissett to the three Claydons (Middle, East,
and Steeple) in winter, marvelling at the change that had
come upon the land since last I was there in summer.

The walk itself begins from Buckingham, where you must
take the road that bears sharp left from the square, sign-
posted to Gawcott. The first half of this mile is agreeable; the second, not so; once more the old, old story of
ancient versus modern.

79

CHRISTMAS MORNING

Many fine old houses flank the left of the way, and there
also are innumerable of those alleys and by-ways and be-
nighted *culs-de-sac* that adorn small country towns, where
the visitor will find many antiquated cottages.   These,
they assure me, are dark and dingy and altogether insani-
tary; yet, how mellow and gracious and crazily symmetrical
they stand, utterly beyond our modern scope either to
conceive or to execute—though not indeed to desire, else
why have you and I come here, at such trouble, to gaze
upon them—

> whose whitened walls were raised in Tudor days,
> and girt by timbers planted in the years
> when Mass was said within the church's nave.

A stately Prebend House is to be seen on the right, and
upon the left a row of Pisa-esque dwellings.   Even the
shunting-yards beyond Buckingham terminus have a charm,
since the station there is neither modern nor industrial, but
consists for the most part of pigs in trucks, and tractors on
bogeys, and gay blue harrows bound with sacking.   Here,
too, are gaitered farmers, highly polished as to cheeks and
toe-cap, cherubically astute, wide of girth, broad of beam,
immense of smile; drawling, curt, dry; grumbling always
of the weather; praising the Liberals, cursing the Social-
ists, voting Conservative.   With them are unmistakable
farmers' wives, colossally unglamorous, unbelievably stal-
wart, magnificent mothers, no-nonsense girls of an inde-
finite vintage, bonneted, bronzed, and rougeless.   Here also
are engines whose vintage is of a similar indefiniteness,
their ponderousness of dome, and wide-eyed whimsicality of
port-hole, suggesting brief encounters in Edwardian years.
    There is a very potent, indefinable attraction about these
small country stations, and especially about their shunting
yards.   It is impressive, of course, to stand at some London
terminus and to watch the crates marked Edinburgh, Ply-

THE MANOR HOUSE, BUCKINGHAM.

mouth, or Belfast; but these are impersonal: they cannot
touch us. For people, on the other hand, who live in a
village, there is a sort of legitimate curiosity in seeing a
package of china arrive for the Vicarage, and two new book-
cases for the Manse, and a bright blue motor-mower for the
Hall. There is a personal interest, too, in the crate of live
geese that is being carried a few stations down the single
line—say, to Steeple Claydon—and one may well muse
upon the contents of the trunk (marked Singapore), now
on the last lap of its journey across the world, bound for the
remoteness of Lenborough, where the historian Gibbon was
lord of the manor. I wonder also at the engine-driver
himself, usually a grizzled veteran, leaning, wisp in hand,
out of the small cab. Is he an express-man put out to grass,

there, on a single by-lane, to dream of past glories; or is he one who never made his grade and has been forever destined to dream of record runs while his own slow-goods plods sedately through uneventful fields and among unrecorded villages?

Gawcott, the first port-of-call, is a scattered hamlet with two inns and two churches, one of the latter having been destroyed long ago, so that the purist will say that Gawcott has not two churches at all, but only one. The houses here are Georgian, Anne, and Tudor. Gilbert Scott, the architect, was a Gawcott man.

Chausecote belonged to the Bishop of Lincoln at the time of Domesday (in the Middle Ages the entire County lay within that diocese, whose bishops at one time had their

A TYPICAL NORTH BUCKINGHAMSHIRE COTTAGE, PRESTON BISSETT

IN HILLESDEN CHURCH

palace at Dorchester, across the border into Oxfordshire). Court-leets of the manor of Prebend-End-cum-Gawcott were held so late as the seventeenth century.   Church Lane leads to the site of the ancient chapel, dedicated to Saint Catherine, now utterly razed.   The present church was built by a local tradesman in 1806.

At the far end of the village, on the left, is the oldest " New Inn " that I have yet seen, its sign standing on the road, upon a mound of grass.   Make for this inn, pass it, eventually, on your left, and proceed for 200 yards, beyond some white cottages, until a lane—Cow Lane—turns sharply left, up a small rise and thence into a meadow.

Turn right here, following the right-hand hedge until, at the left corner of the next field, your path crosses rightward over a fence, with one well-worn stone for surer footing. Make across this field, steering for two tall trees, and leaving Lenborough Wood on your right flank.   Here the path twists left in order to avoid a hayrick and a pond.   The going thereafter is easy and well defined; you simply follow your nose, as they say, leaving Lenborough Wood behind you, on the right, and crossing three fields (keep to their left hedge) until you come upon the road.

Lenborough, meanwhile, is no more than a collection of cottages and detached farms.   For many years it belonged to the Ingoldsbys, but during the eighteenth century passed to the Gibbons, of whom one, the historian Edward, being lord of this manor in 1735, pulled down the ancient house and gave one wing of the remnants to his tenant.   One supposes that he knew Lenborough as a youth, when he had obeyed as a son and sighed as a lover, but the historian of Buckinghamshire will read Gibbon's *Autobiography* in vain for any record of Lenborough.   The truth is, Gibbon's paternal estates lay in Hampshire, and his own rustic rambles, such as they were, confined themselves to that

G

STEEPLE CLAYDON
CHURCH

HARVEST-TIME AT
STEEPLE CLAYDON

County.   He was, in fact, a Captain of the Hampshire Militia.   His service was a respite from his delvings in " the mud of Arian Controversy ", and, as he admitted in his memoirs, " the Captain of the Hampshire grenadiers . . . has not been useless to the historian of Rome ".   The discipline and drills " gave me a clear notion of the phalanx and legion ".

Just before joining the road you will pass along a few yards of grassy track, and beyond that, on the outskirts of Preston Bissett, you will see a small and delightful hold-ing with a barn and thatched cottage.   This, blessedly, is inhabited, but the large numbers of similar holdings that are not inhabited, or that have been given over to the week-ends of business-men, recalls Goldsmith's solemn warning:

> A time there was, ere England's griefs began,
> When every rood of ground maintained its man;
> But times are altered; trade's unfeeling train
> Usurp the land and dispossess the swain.

A little beyond this small farm stands " The White Hart Inn ", thatched, cream-washed, timbered, a picture come to life, being stone-flagged and beech-warmed; in summer cool, and in winter a blaze of aromatic cordiality.

Here indeed is a place where:

> High climbs the smoke, in ringlets slow and blue:
> bright burns the lamp on ruddy-gleaming hue
> of country faces and of country hands:
> calm is the rustic mien, as though the sands
> of Time stood still, and would not slip away.
> They talk their talk—of harvest and of grain—
> in ancient accent, and compute their gain
> in bushel, hayrick, barnful, harvest home,
> the language of great Domesday's massive tome.

The name Preston Bissett is a corruption of *Villa Presby-teri*, or *Priest's Town*; the Bissett having come from a family that lived here during the Middle Ages. In 1066 the manor was held by Odo, Bishop of Bayeux, and for many years afterwards by the Bissetts.

Apart from a vivid rash of pink council houses—mercifully, a small rash—Preston Bissett is unspoiled. It has a second old inn, called " The Old Hat ", and a splendid church standing on a ridge above the roadway. In this church you will find some magnificent *sedilia*, and a gallery in the very best manner of the early eighteenth century. There are three *piscinae*—one in the chancel, and one in each aisle. Near the altar is a coffin-shaped slab dated in the fourteenth century.

You are fairly high up here, as heights go in the north of this County, but the next footpath dips gently into lower land. Just behind " The Old Hat " you will find a path that leads from the village in a south-easterly direction. It crosses a by-lane after ten minutes or so, and continues straight on, over a stream, until it becomes a track and enters the hamlet of Hillesden. As you walk you will see the high ground of Oving away to your right, and the trees of Charndon Wood nearly 400 feet up. You are here in the very heart of unoccupied Buckinghamshire. You may, if you care, test the solitude by shouting at the top of your voice. If any man hears you I shall be surprised (and so, of course, will he).

Although I have lived in the country—and in this countryside—since I was a boy, and have tried farming for myself, *in statu pupillarii*, I am still amazed at the apparent perennial absence of labourers from our fields. For weeks on end, it seems, the fields are empty, and although *some-body* has come to lay the new hedge, and plough the old stubble, he seems to work as Jack Frost works, invisibly and amid eternal silence. Sometimes during my walks hereabouts I catch sight of a weatherbeaten cap, but it is

THATCHING AT EAST
CLAYDON

A FINE OLD HOMESTEAD
IN STEEPLE CLAYDON

SEPTEMBER IN THE CLAYDON COUNTRY

always in the far field: and when by chance I come upon a
circle of charred wood, showing where the hedger has been,
it is always yesterday's embers that are stirred by the
winter wind.

Hillesden is the scene of one of the most exciting incidents
of the Civil Wars. Hillesden House was then owned by
a loyal gentleman, Sir Alexander Denton, who decided to
fortify the place as a bastion between the opposing armies,
the King's forces lying at Oxford, and the Parliament's at
Newport Pagnell. Sir Alexander established contact with
Oxford by means of a chain of horsemen and runners, with
posts at Twyford, Bicester, Chesterton, and Bletchington.
He then began to build several barns and stables around the
house, intending to fill them with earth, but was attacked

while the work was still in progress. Having only five small cannon, and a troop of cavalry supported by 150 foot soldiers, he seemed an easy prey for the forces under Colonel Cromwell. The first assault, however, was gallantly repulsed, and the discomfited Roundheads returned into Newport Pagnell to recover from the shock. A large army was then sent to the attack, and the house surrounded. After a fierce skirmish, in which the Royalists were hopelessly outnumbered, the handful of survivors emerged, as they imagined, into honourable captivity. They were in fact either hanged from trees, or marched away, despite their wounds and fatigue, to the village of Padbury.

The church is a wonderful example of Perpendicular. The footpath out of Hillesden passes Churchill Farm and begins to descend, through pleasant meadow-land, to Claydon Plank Farm, crossing a stream this side of the outbuildings. You are now in the country of the Claydons and in a county of fair names:

> The fingerposts of England
> make native melodies
> pointing impartial courses
> to hidden Arcadies . . .
> Bix and Brill and Russell's Water,
> Weston Underwood,
> Preston Bissett, Christmas Common,
> Willen, Robin Hood,
> Claydons (Middle, East, and Steeple)
> Summer Heath and Speen,
> Brickhills (Bow and Great and Little)
> Lee and Lacey Green.

Since there are three Claydons, and since moreover they are chapters in the story of a family that is itself a chapter of English history, the reader will not expect to receive a full account of the places. The most that we can hope to do is to give a bare outline of the fascinating intimate

IN MID-BUCKINGHAMSHIRE, OVERLOOKING BLEDLOW RIDGE AND THE VALE OF AYLESBURY

history that is written upon every stick and stone and stile of the neighbourhood.

When you have entered the village of Steeple Claydon you will suspect that the " authorities " have not heard of the place, for it still lacks either council-houses or red-bricked community centres.   Instead you will see some of the finest timbered and thatched cottages that are in England to-day, and an imposing church, from whose porch a wide view opens across the plain toward Aylesbury.

The manor of Steeple Claydon belonged to the King in 1066, but was presented by Henry I to his mistress, Edith Forne, in 1120, as a part of her marriage dowry when she became the wife of Robert D'Oyley.   This couple founded Oseney Abbey, near Oxford.   Strangely enough, and having passed through many noble families, the manor again became part of a Queen's dowry, this time of Katherine of Aragon.   In 1554 the manor was bestowed by Queen Mary upon Sir Thomas Chaloner, one of the few English Knights that were created by an official other than the Sovereign, Chaloner having been knighted on the field of Musselburgh by the Protector Somerset.   In the early eighteenth century the village was bought by the Verney family.   (They were an ancient family, and pronounced the name *Varney*.)

The original manor house was pulled down, and a successor built, by the Verneys' agent; its name, Oliver's Camp, is a relic of the siege of Hillesden House, which we have noted already.   On a building near the church a tablet was set up bearing the words: " The Camp Barn.   Around this spot the Army of Parliament under the command of Cromwell, was encamped March 1644, and on the 3rd of that month advanced from hence to the attack on Hillesden House."

The Church of Saint Michael has been enlarged recently,

though not spoiled, except by a hideous and huge organ, occupying space that should be a lady-chapel, and for centuries very probably was a lady-chapel. Part of a *piscina* may be seen in the south wall, and, opposite, an *ambry*.

The other Claydons are best reached by road. The way is pleasant enough, for on the right stands the high ground of Oving, and far to the left, the roofs of Buckingham. Cross the single-line railway after a few moments, and bear sharply left and right with the lane.

Middle Claydon—so called from its position between Steeple Claydon and East Botolph, or Botolph Claydon—is linked with the family of Verney, and in Saxon times was held by Alwin, a thane of Edward the Confessor. Five centuries ago the manor was bought by Sir Ralph Verney, Knight, Alderman, Lord Mayor of London in 1465, and Member of Parliament for London in the following year. To trace the history of this family is to trace, and to a certain extent to understand also, the history of England, from her status as a small island, through her hey-day as the greatest nation in the world, and at length, by way of the Industrial Revolution, to her transformation into a nation of shop-keepers and machine-minders.

Sir Ralph Verney, who bought the lands here, was a descendant of John de Verney, lord of the manor of Fleet Marston in the early thirteenth century. Thereafter and until modern times, a Verney has always been to the fore in English affairs. Edmund, Ralph's son, was Sheriff of Hertfordshire; the second son of this Edmund was Knight Marshal in 1632 and gallant Standard-bearer to the King at Edgehill. Sir Edmund's body was never found after the battle—only his hand, still grasping the Royal Standard. A ring that was found on one of his fingers contained a portrait of the King, and has been preserved by

THE TRACK TO
OVING

THE AUTHOR,
AND BILL, AT
GREAT
WOOLSTONE

the family. Sir Ralph, Edmund's son, who was created Baronet at the Restoration, outlived his own heir and his grandchildren. His second son was created Baron Verney of Belturbet, County Cavan, by Queen Anne, and later a Viscount.

In time the male line died out and a female Verney was created Baroness Fermanagh in the Kingdom of Ireland. She, too, died without heir, whereupon the title became extinct and the lands passed once again to a female relative, whose issue took the family name. There is not space here to describe the wonderful art treasures in the Verneys' house, but reference may be made to the Verney Papers, issued by the Camden Society, in which much intimate history will be found.

Every feature in this village is worthy of notice: from the church—whose chancel, as the Latin inscription tells us, was built by Roger and Mary Giffard in 1519—to the excellent inn and the serried ranks of white cottages, a joy to the eye and an assurance to the spirit, impassive spectators of so much history, patient beneath the strokes of time and chance, the homes of men who lived in greater and happier days.

Hard by the Townsend Farm a footpath will take you into East Claydon, which you may well find the choicest of the trio, together with its small appanage, Botolph Claydon. (It is interesting to note, in passing, that the Claydons were the first English villages to possess a Public Library, which they achieved during the second half of the nineteenth century.)

The manor of East Claydon belonged to Geoffrey de Mandeville, Constable of the Tower of London, at the Conquest, and passed through an unusually large number of families until it was bought by Viscount Verney, for £25,790, in 1729.

GREAT MISSENDEN, THE CHURCH AND COTTAGES

A descendant of this Geoffrey was also Constable of the Tower, under King Stephen, but took to highway robbery with a band of forty desperate horsemen, and was killed by an arrow during a skirmish with the royal troops in Suffolk. As an ex-communicate he was denied Christian burial; but the Knights Templars carried his body to London, where they placed it in a coffin, which they set in the branches of a tree in the Temple Garden, where it remained for twenty years—until Pope Alexander II gave permission for its burial before the west door of the Temple Church.

In the middle of the village you will see a farmhouse that is the remains of a stone mansion belonging to the Abells, whose arms are carved there in stone, impaled by the Verney arms also. The fact that Bernwood Forest stretched here from Brill, is proved by the name of Bernwood, a small tract of trees, in the parish.

From Botolph Claydon, which is an extension of East Claydon, there is a magnificent view leftward from the road, towards Oving and Whitchurch, three or four miles to the south-east. This, surely, is living refutation of my aforementioned Grampian friend, and of " those noodles " (to use Browning's phrase) who still believe that northern Buckinghamshire is a dreary expanse of flat land, stale, dull, and unprofitable. Mark well the girth of the oaks that arise from the meadows, and of the elms that wait upon the skyline. Innumerable small streams glitter blue in the sunlight; and ahead, not above half a mile distant, is the richly-wooded country of Greatmoor, with Charndon Wood, Sheephouse Wood, Home Wood, Decoypond Wood, and half a dozen others. Their names delight the ear, and their leaves declare the season.

From Botolph Claydon you may proceed for one mile, along the Grandborough road, to Grandborough Station, whence a branch line will carry you into Winslow, on the

Aylesbury road, or into Aylesbury itself.   You may, if you prefer, return into Steeple Claydon, where the line will take you to Buckingham.

I can warmly recommend a journey along this branch line; and I hope that one day somebody will write an account of a journey through England by these single-line tracks. Certain formalities are observed—for instance, the boiler must be filled with water, and the furnace kept going, but the total impression of such a journey is not formal at all. Level-crossings, hereabouts, become the scenes of long talk between crew and station-hand, starting, as a rule, with the potato prospects, but frequently concluding with an analysis of the political situation in the Balkans, as it affects Grandborough.   Here, on the branch line, you will find the real England.

CHAPTER SIX

FROM DINTON AND BIGG'S CAVE, THROUGH UPPER AND
NETHER WINCHENDON, TO CUDDINGTON AND CHEARS-
LEY. (ABOUT 10 MILES)

OUR starting-point, Dinton, is reached by motor-bus from
the market town of Thame, or from Aylesbury and Oxford.
The stop is at Dinton Castle, a peculiarly unconvincing
mound of stones arrayed in a sour disorder by Sir John
Vanhatten in 1769, for what purpose is uncertain.

Take the left of the two cross-roads, through 200 yards of
elm avenue, and proceed right-handed at the next crossing,
by the church and the Hall; thence into Dinton village,
leaving the Hall on your left.

Dinton has always seemed to me to be one of the loveliest
villages of the plain, an Auburn sweet indeed, tallying
closely with Goldsmith's full fond catechism:

> Dear lovely bowers of innocence and ease,
> Seats of my youth, when every sport could please,
> How often have I loitered o'er thy green,
> Where humble happiness endeared each scene:
> How often have I paused on every charm,
> The sheltered cot, the cultivated farm,
> The never-failing brook, the busy mill,
> The decent church that topped the neighbouring hill.

If a man has lived long and happily in a place, and finds
that his own life-story is engraven upon the hills and the
fields thereof, it sometimes happens that he tends not
indeed to exaggerate the beauty of those scenes, but rather
to pass them off lightly, like the quiet manner of his breathing
or the sound of his own voice, so much have they become
a part of himself. If therefore I have in any way fallen
short of a just account of these Buckinghamshire villages,

it will have been through my habit of unconsciously taking them for granted. Against this grisly process of time there is no sure remedy. The best that a man may hope for is, that absence, or the threat of absence, shall from time to time recover him to his senses, and reveal to him the full glory of the beauty that by day and night he has taken too easily for granted. The mean, perhaps, lies mid-way between a thoughtless negligence and a too-conscious clinging to the vanished past and a fleeting present.

Dinton, at all events, a village with some history to its credit, was one of the manors presented by the Conqueror to his half-brother, Odo Bishop of Bayeux, who held also 184 lordships in Kent, and elsewhere 255. Like Wolsey after him, this fighting prelate aspired to become Pope, and having purchased a castle in Rome he prepared to set sail thither, with a fleet of ships, from the Isle of Wight, but was detained and imprisoned, on the eve of his departure, by the King. After a chequered and treasonous career, he died at Palermo.

During the seventeenth century Dinton—by now, *Donyngton*—passed to the Mayne family, of whom Simon, Justice of the Peace, was one of the judges that under Bradshaw's presidency unlawfully condemned King Charles I to death. At the Restoration Mayne was fortunate to escape with his life. The Hall, of Jacobean style, very large and mellow and trim, often concealed Simon Mayne from marauding Royalists. In its upper storey he built a secret hiding-place of three stairs which, when they had been lifted, revealed a tunnel lined with cloth, whence he would crawl to safety.

Having passed Dinton Hall, the lane bends sharply left and right; and at the point where it bends right, stands an ancient cottage, called Bigg's Cave, very well cared-for to-day. In this historic house I have spent many happy hours on my way between the Vale and the Hills. As the poet says:

> Down to the Vale land I will go,
> where the cattle idle slow
> through the marshy meadows
> and beside the willows.
>
> Down to Dinton, let it be,
> where the stream twines leisurely
> always seeking, winding,
> never, never finding.
>
> Down from beeches on the hills,
> down among the polished rills
> and a lowly plain
> burdened by the grain.
>
> Far behind, the Chilterns lie
> silhouetted on the sky
> —wood and winter wheat,
> green and grey and neat.

This homestead is the site of Bigg's Cave and is marked upon the Ordnance map. John Bigg was secretary to Simon Mayne, and himself reputed (though inaccurately) to have executed the King. At the Restoration John Bigg grew melancholy mad, probably of an anxiety neurosis, and led the life of a hermit—a fact that is borne out by " The Hermit Inn " at Stone, a mile away. Bigg, at all events, rarely emerged from his cave, save during the summer months, when he was seen much among the woods of Kimble, at the foot of the Chilterns, five miles off. Bigg's method of mending his clothes—he never changed them—was simple. He simply sewed a patch over the hole. His boots, of which one is preserved at the Hall, were similarly treated, and at his death were said to have ten layers of leather upon them.

It is worth while to explore this village and to sample

the by-lanes at its far end, for their cottages and gardens, and the fine old inn there.   In the background, distant on the skyline, the Chiltern Hills keep immemorial vigil over the Vale.   They are indeed the Hounds of Heaven, and for many miles there is no escaping them, nor any desire to do so.

Having tasted what Dinton has to offer—and, not least, the superb tympanum of the church's Norman entrance—you should return, by the same way, to the egregious Dinton Castle, a few yards beyond which a track leads leftward into the fields.

Follow the footpath that soon veers left from this track, sloping gently into the valley of the Thame.   The river is there to guide you, down on your left, and for higher land-mark, 333 feet above the sea, the ancient buildings of Beachendon Farm glow in the sunlight, or peer obstinately through the gloom, timbered and thatched Christophers to guide a lost traveller.

After perhaps half a mile of low-lying meadows the foot-path joins with a by-lane that has branched leftward from the main Aylesbury highroad.   Having reached this lane you turn left, across a couple of small bridges and past a most musical weir, until, as the lane veers sharply right, you see the cart-track leading from the left to Beachendon Farm.   A few yards farther along, and on the same side of the lane, a footpath strikes clean across the rising fields and will carry you into Upper Winchendon.

On reaching the road you turn to the left, and after a few moments' walking will find yourself in the centre of the hamlet, whose ancient church can be seen among trees on the right.   At Upper Winchendon you are on the crest of a narrow ridge, with glorious views on either side.   To your right, across the roofs of Waddesdon, lie the Forest of Yardley, and Northamptonshire's southern border.   To

BIGG'S CAVE, DINTON

ON DINTON GREEN

DINTON FOLLY

your left, across Whiteleaf and Princes Risborough, stand the Chilterns, with many a fair village in the valley below. Upper Winchendon has views indeed; but it is Nether, or Lower, Winchendon that is the lovelier of these two hamlets, and to Nether Winchendon we will hasten.

The way lies through the Upper village, past a fine farm-house on your left, called " The Limes ".   At " The Limes " you may, if you care, take the footpath that dips steeply leftward into the valley; or, if the going is heavy that day, you may follow the road.   The path is the more attractive; but the lane, too, is worth the walking, since it winds about a deep, green valley, and at length enters Nether Winchendon a few yards from the church.

There are, of course, many English hamlets more

beautiful than Nether Winchendon, but I cannot at the moment recall them. I believe that one building only in all the place—a small, decent school—is less than three hundred years old; many of them are early Tudor; the church is medieval. Besides its fine Jacobean pulpit and some ancient timber pews (these latter stand immediately below the musicians' gallery), the Church of Saint Nicholas is remarkable in that a nineteenth-century restoration did not mar it. On the contrary, the modern raftered roof, resting well upon plain corbals, is in excellent taste, and in certain lights may deceive the inexpert eye into taking it for thrice its age.

The name Winchendon is a blend of two Anglo-Saxon

NETHER WINCHENDON PRIORY

LOOKING TOWARDS BUCKINGHAM, FROM GREEN HAILEY

nouns, *wychen*, meaning springs, and *don*, meaning a hillock. As you enter the village by footpath, the leftward lane will take you past Winchendon Priory, the principal house, a sandwich of Tudor, Jacobean, and mullioned Prince Albert.   At one time this Priory belonged to the Abbey of Notley.

Returning past the church, you see on your right a part of the seat of the ancient Knolly family, a splendid brick-and-timber homestead, now a farmhouse, very weather-beaten and hale; not caring overmuch for anything at all; a shade cynical as to the benefits of social revolution; and (since homes have souls) a little homesick also, on account of the happier and more robust era into which it was born.

Whenever I am in Nether Winchendon I give thanks that it will outlive me, to be a joy and an inspiration to countless Englishmen yet unborn:

> Not in my time, O Lord, let these decay,
> these sturdy English men of horse and hay,
> of plough and harrow, hive and paved dairy
> —the manor and its lord, trim-clipped from view,
> the quiet church wherein from week to week
> is preached, and practised too, such simple creed
> as all men may observe for all men's good:
> the measured, lazy lilt of Chiltern tone,
> all undefiled by culture or the twang
> of hybrid jargon from a newer world.

Follow this lane through the village, past the disused entrance to the Priory—an entrance, alas, so like to that of Lord Marshmallow's scarcely-paid-for seat down at Hogs-norton, whose gates, as Mr. Gillie Potter has recounted for us, are held together partly, it is true, by the awareness of a fine old English tradition, but partly also, and perhaps chiefly, by a less ancient and a more tangible force—rope.

A few yards beyond these gates, and still to the left of the lane, you must join a footpath that begins between some

FEBRUARY SUNSHINE IN THE WOODS AT LITTLE HAMPDEN

NETHER WINCHENDON, FROM THE CHURCH TOWER

fine old cottages. This is clearly marked by an oak standing on the verge of the road. Pause to admire these cottages, for they are festooned with a most healthy rime of lichen, moss, and creeper, and their profuse thatch wears crazy list, very deceptive to an eye attuned to the puny symmetry of a pre-fabricated home, for that list was old when James II cast the Great Seal into the river, and will outlive by many decades the unclean rash of modern villas that has besmirched England—

> the cemetery . . .
> that sprawls unleashed across a countryside
> where Cockneys build their cut-price palaces.

The path enters a small gate, where it turns leftward for a few yards and then veers rightward over the Thame. To your left is a good view of the Priory and its private bridge; behind, the highway from Upper Winchendon makes a pleasing prospect against the sky; ahead, the spire of Cuddington Church, and the roofs of the cottages there, cast summer shadows over the still meadowland.   The footpath here is well-shod and raised against a river that between November and March is often in flood.

Cuddington you enter through the disused gates of an older drive to the Priory, but these at least have been spared the modern indignity of string and nettles; and no bucolic cryptics are scrawled chalkily and cheekily and ungrammatically upon their lichened features.

I have never been able to prefer one of these two villages above the other.   Nether Winchendon is the more truly medieval, and its deep silence is perhaps one semitone

IN NETHER WINCHENDON

FROM NETHER
WINCHENDON CHURCH
PATH

INTERIOR, NETHER
WINCHENDON CHURCH;
JACOBEAN PULPIT ON
THE RIGHT

EXTERIOR, NETHER
WINCHENDON CHURCH

more profound than Cuddington's; but Cuddington has some splendid cottages, and, by reason of its more apparent inhabitants, conveys a livelier impression of reality. Nether Winchendon might easily *be* a picture; Cuddington is at least a *moving* picture.

Cuddington, at all events, has an ancient past. William gave the manor to Lanfranc, his saintly Archbishop of Canterbury; and afterwards it passed into the Buckingham-shire family of Tyringham, who held, and still hold, lands in the northern parts of the County.

Although the Church of Saint Nicholas was restored in 1852, it was not ruined thereby. Minton's glazed paving-stones (diamond lozenge) will not be to everyone's liking, but the arching and an ancient font prevail.

To the south of the parish, just below Dadbrook House, runs a stream that formerly was famous for its " medicinal properties ".

Born and bred in Cuddington was James Holyman, second Bishop of Bristol, who spoke and wrote zealously in defence of the Catholic faith, and more especially against the King's divorce from Katherine of Aragon. The house in which he was born stands to-day, and seems to be a very prosperous farmstead.

An earlier incumbent of this parish invested the sum of £600 in Government stock, the interest to be spent annually in January upon coals for the poor.

Those who wish to rejoin the Aylesbury highway at this point may do so by following the lane signposted to Dinton, bearing left at the road junction outside the village.

Those who wish to continue for another mile or two may take the right-handed of these two roads, into Gibraltar. This lane offers another vivid contrast between the two major types of Buckinghamshire landscape—the Vale and the Hills—for it meanders drowsily among elm, oak, and willow (those sure heralds of a marshy soil) above which, stretching along the entire length of skyline, the Chilterns make strong outline, dipping slightly at each extremity. Above Whiteleaf the hills rise steeply, cupping, on the other side, the still and secluded hamlets of Great and Little Hampden, those superannuated sires of English history in general and of an aristocratic Whiggery in particular; and, after these, the hill village of Prestwood, mile upon mile of unravished quietude, whose hills rise and fall in interlocking spurs, soft and fruitful as breasts, most gently strong; a little realm void of towns, and unknown by the motor-bus; a good deed shining brightly through the naughty world; in brief, my home.

Gibraltar is a gathering of old cottages leavened by some houses that are neither cottages nor old. From here the motor-bus will take you into Aylesbury or Thame or Oxford.

If it is a long summer's day, and you are out to see as much as you comfortably can, the hamlet of Chearsley is worth a

THE INN AT GIBRALTAR

visit.   A footpath leads westward thither from behind the inn.   From this path also the same contrast is to be seen— hill and plain, seemingly miles from anywhere, with sometimes a lone figure in far field, a hedger gloved and sacked, standing in meditation before the charred white circles of his day's work:

> Lone on a desert island in the fields,
> far from the sight of home or sound of voice,
> he bent above the hedge, and hacked a way
> lithesome and trim athwart the tousled hazel.
> With tender-callous stroke he snicked each shoot
> justly, with such a stroke as cleft the bark
> yet left the tissues touching, that their lips,
> though gaping, drew the immemorial sap.
> Thus bent and humbled, fashioned to his will,
> and neatly twined and plaited to his eye,
> the sickled twigs yet lived and yet would sprout
> sturdy, but pre-ordained in woof and warp.
> Full half a mile of hedge the man had trimmed,
> and in his wake, as evidence of toil,
> charred circles of white wood adorned the field,
> one crackling yet, and worried by the wind.

Chearsley is an ancient small place whose name is derived from a corruption of *Cerdicerleah*, of the Saxon Chronicle, where Cerdic and Cymric defeated the Britons.   Skeletons are still ploughed up here, but these, I think, are not of so great an age, being more likely the grim relics of a feudal gallows that once stood in the hamlet.

Despite its uninviting porch, the church—again of Saint Nicholas—has several good features.   In the centre of the chancel are some brasses.   It may be necessary to remove the drugget in order to see these.   Such removal does not constitute sacrilege, provided that it is done carefully and the brasses duly re-covered.

From Chearsley to the Aylesbury road should not take many minutes' walking.   The way is agreeable.

I

The careful observer will have noted already some of the features of the soil hereabouts.   The number of oaks and elms and willows along the way is a sure sign of the clayey land upon which such trees thrive.   Beeches, on the other hand, do best on the chalky land of the Chilterns and are less in evidence here in the plain.   It was this dearth of beeches around Buckingham that seemed to disprove those antiquaries who derived the County's name from the Saxon word *boc*, meaning beech tree.   The *ham*, or home, among such *boc*, or beech, would scarcely fit the scenery around Buckingham, where oak and elm abound, but not the beech.

From time to time in these walks the wayfarer will come across a curious outcrop of sandy soil, more typical of

AT CHEARSLEY

Surrey than of Buckinghamshire.   Such regions are dotted willy-nilly about the County—most notably along the Bedfordshire border at Woburn and the three Brickhills, but also at Ibstone and upon the common of Turville Heath, across the Oxfordshire border.   There is a small tract of this soil on Little Hampden Common also, where gorse flourishes. As a rule, however, the northern and plain lands of Buckinghamshire are clayey, very heavy to work when lying by river or stream.   Near Olney, on the Northamptonshire border, I once ploughed a February field that needed three strong horses to work the share.   Yet, even on this clay, a solitary hillock of chalk is to be found, and in the Chilterns the bottoms, or valleys, often reveal a clay subsoil.

CHAPTER SEVEN

FROM BRILL, THROUGH LUDGERSHALL, KINGSWOOD, GREN-
DON UNDERWOOD, AND WOODHAM, TO WADDESDON.
(ABOUT 10 MILES)

BRILL, the starting-point of this walk, is a sequestered
village high on a hill. Motor-buses reach it from Thame
and Aylesbury; and a single-line railway, of the sort already
noticed, runs here from Princes Risborough, but the
station lies some way out of the village.

Brill being of an historic interest far out of proportion to
its present size or importance, deserves some attention. The
village itself is windswept and exposed, standing on the
crest of a hill, nearly 700 feet up, and only a short walk from
the Oxfordshire border. Seen from the old windmill here,
the hills of Warwickshire and of Gloucestershire wait clear
against the sky, England in little lying lovely below.

Brill has a splendid windmill, which for some years was
allowed to fall into a state of disgraceful ruin, and very
likely it would by now have toppled down, a mass of
timbers, had not the Buckinghamshire Archaeological
Society made itself responsible for its welfare. America,
with its vast territory, has nevertheless taken enormous
tracts under its wing, and every old building there is
jealously maintained. Englishmen, it seems—save for the
minority—prefer to build new garages and cinemas.

Follow the road leading through the village towards
Buckingham. Follow it for about 300 yards, bearing right
at the first set of cross-roads, where the way dips between
common lands grazed by village stock. At the foot of this
incline, and to the left of the road, stands a signpost; and

to the left of the post, by some farm buildings, you will see a stile. Cross this stile and make for the right-handed of two elms at the far end of the field.

From time immemorial—back, indeed, to Mercian days—Brill has been associated with the Kings of England. Edward the Confessor came here during the hunting season, to enjoy the chase in Bernwood Forest. Henry II kept Court here, and with him came his worldly Chancellor, Thomas à Becket. King John arrived here on October 23rd, 1203, and spent that Christmas in the place. Henry III resided here often. And all this glory is as though it had never been, for Brill to-day is one of the sleepiest places under the sun, not a whit more wide awake than Housman's Shropshire hamlets. Even the local industry, pottery, has forsaken it, though there is one woman here who can still make " real " lace. Gone, too, is Shirley Brooks, jovial editor and last of the original staff of *Punch*, who was born here in 1816. One wonders whether, amid the smoke and haste and intrigue of London life, he found time to close his eyes and to imagine Brill and its small universe of tilth, thatch, and spire? In this green and pleasant land, then, the English Kings once held their Court, and to picture their pomp and circumstance is an agreeable indulgence.

Meanwhile the footpath awaits us—straight across meadows whose regular grooves are relics of a primitive system of ploughing that sought to drain these marshy fields.

Soon the footpath crosses an ancient track and enters through a gate at the corner of Rushbeds Wood. This wood it skirts for about half a mile, leaving it always on the right. Various inviting gates lead into Rushbeds Wood, and upon a warm day a visit is its own reward, for although the trees have been thinned too severely, the place is still a wood, where primrose and wood anemone sparkle like jewels beneath the oaks.　Here indeed you will be far from the crowd's strife, and that is sometimes a boon.

I was here last on a mild evening of spring, a time of promises that have never yet been broken; and as I reluctantly moved onward in the early gloaming, I thought that Blake had written the perfect epitaph to my merely personal—yet utterly universal—experience:

> Farewell, green fields and happy groves,
>   Where flocks have took delight,
> Where lambs have nibbled, silent moves
>   The feet of angels bright.
>   Unseen they pour blessing,
>   And joy without ceasing,
>   On each bud and blossom,
>   And each sleeping bosom.

The path comes suddenly upon a railway, which it crosses by winding over the mouth of a tunnel.　At the far side, turn sharp leftward and make for the bridge, 200 yards away, from which a track bears right, down a fine avenue of elms and thence on to the road.

Turn left at this road, along a mile of pleasant country lane whose hedges and ditches are models of good husbandry, and proof of what Buckinghamshire men can do.　Here, at its simplest and most remote, is typical north Bucks landscape—gentle slopes, massive oaks, elms aloof in far fields, thatched cottage, distant hillock, and—pervading them all—the presence of innumerable quiet meadows, stretching, as it seems, to the world's end, tokens of a patriarchal squirearchy and of an independent yeomanry, the very antithesis to modern life as it is lived by the majority of English men and women and, alas, children.

To see the children at play in these fields is to feel most poignantly the cynical paradox of the Industrial Revolution and its contemporary harvest of urban and mechanized

THE CANAL AT GREAT LINFORD

mass-existence, the nightmare caricature of mankind's gregarious instinct.

> In drab and samely streets they dwell,
> eternal Death, eternal Hell,
> or herd like sheep in skyward blocks
> of stone, like city-frightened flocks.

The hamlet of Ludgershall is no fit place for a poet to linger in, since it stirs within him the very well-springs of wonder and gratitude and loving-kindness, and thereby renders him doubly vulnerable to the gibes of urban scoffers and to the mood of the majority in his own times. Ludgershall's outriders are a pair of decent labourers' cottages, very neat and compact; but the spirit of the place declares itself

WINTER IN NORTH BUCKINGHAMSHIRE

more truly in the whitewashed and steeply-thatched homestead that stands on the right of the lane, where it bends
sharply, and by a venerable farm, a little beyond the cottage
and to its left, whose beasts browse placidly on the pasture
that dips in emerald mounds to the brim of the lane. You
must carry past these, bearing right, over a small bridge,
until, 200 yards ahead, you come upon the village green.

The sight of Ludgershall on a bright May morning, or
toward nightfall in December, after a fall of snow, is a cure
for all of life's petty irkings, and balm for all save its most
bitter sorrows. And yet, after all, this is a simple place—
merely a hotch-potch of Tudor and Caroline cottages
draped willy-nilly about a topsy-turvy green, where beasts
browse, and children play, and old men mourn the time's
decadence, no doubt as their forefathers mourned it when
John Wicliffe was vicar here.

The mass of great names in English history are country-
bred, born among meadows or upon hills, destined to
remember throughout the distractions of fame, and to their
life's end, the seasons' passing, and the talk of old men in
tap-rooms. From end to end of England are villages and
hamlets and isolated manor houses that are for ever linked
with the names of great Englishmen—her poets, her sailors,
her soldiers; her artists, statesmen, and scientists. Nor is
this quiet, small place an exception to that happy rule, for
John Wicliffe was priest here from 1368 until 1374, during
which time he wrote his famous theological work, *De
Domini Civili*.

The church, which is dedicated to the Assumption of the
Blessed Virgin, is worthy the association, for, despite several
instances of the process that has been aptly misnamed
" restoration," it contains some splendid Decorated arches,
a transitional Norman font, and several Perpendicular
windows. The sexagonal pulpit is Jacobean.

A CORNER OF
LUDGERSHALL

"HARBOUR LIGHTS",
LUDGERSHALL

ELIZABETHAN COTTAGE,
GRENDON UNDERWOOD

At Domesday the Bishop of Constance held *Lotegasser*. He had previously officiated at the Battle of Hastings, as soldier, on the side of the Duke.

It is tempting to make-believe that John Wicliffe would recognize *Lotegasser* were he to see it to-day; but the truth is, that although the village has changed very little during the past three hundred years, John Wicliffe might well pass through it to-day without at once recognizing his old living, for in those years the three-field system of husbandry prevailed and the greater part of England was forest— that is, waste or uncultivated land, a brigand-ridden and beast-prowled realm of woodland, heath, moor, and cop- pice. In the fourteenth century, moreover, the adjacent forest of Bernwood, where the Kings of England delighted to chase the wild boar, must have stretched very near to *Lotegasser*.

At Ludgershall you must inquire the way, for the foot- path is hard to find. I commend " The Bull and Butcher " as the likeliest source of inspiration. The footpath runs right-handed from behind some cottages, and these cottages cannot easily be described here. Ask for the footpath to Kingswood and Sharp's Hill. There are two such paths out of the village, and it does not matter which of them you take, because they join after a few hundred yards. Before leaving, I advise you to seek out the tiny cottage called " Harbour Lights ", the home of a retired sailor, very snug and maritime.

The path meanders through half a mile of meadow, plough, and copse, leaving Tittershall Wood on its right and sloping gently until it crosses the ancient Akeman Street, at the foot of Sharp's Hill. This Akeman Street, or straight way, which is of a great antiquity, almost certainly a work of the Romans, enters the County west- ward of Tring and leaves it a little to the south of Bicester,

WOUGHTON-ON-THE-GREEN, INN AND CHURCH GATE

across the Oxfordshire border. In its Buckinghamshire
section it was designed to connect *Verulam* (Saint Albans)
with Alchester.

I suggest a detour here, by turning right, along the
Akeman Way, into the village of Kingswood, 300 yards to
the south-east, whose inn is called " The Crooked Billet ".
Kingswood was formerly forest land of Brill parish, but
became appropriated to the Crown, whence its name.
Henry II is said to have built a bower here for his mistress,
Rosamund Clifford, the " fair Rosamund " of song and
ballad. Indeed, an old map of the Forest does in fact show
a lane called " Rosiman's Waye " through a glade. The
hamlet, at all events, belonged to the Mercers Company
until 1812, when it passed to the Duchy of Buckingham and
Chandos, now extinct.

Back again at the foot of Sharp's Hill, a gentle hillock of 288 feet, you may enjoy a splendid view westward to the Cotswolds.

Sharp's Hill Farm, not far off, marks the site of an ancient moated house, once a place of refuge in Bernwood Forest, under the protection of the Knights Hospitallers.

Ten minutes' brisk walking will bring you into Grendon Underwood, whose name derives from Bernwood Forest.

Grendon Underwood was held by a branch of the Ferrers family, whence it passed to Gerard de Braybrooke. And at Grendon, of all places, we come as it were face to face with Shakespeare. The facts of this encounter have been debated by scholars, and as an undergraduate I once passed a tedious, unprofitable afternoon in noting sources for a discussion of this very problem. It seems probable, at all events, that Shakespeare passed the night— perhaps more than once—at " The Ship Inn " here, on his way between London and Stratford on Avon. The inn long ago went out of commission as such, but reappeared as a farmhouse. It stands on the highway, at the western end of the village.

The link with Shakespeare, however, is stronger and more precise than that, for Grendon Wood, half a mile northeast of the place, is very likely the original of the woodland setting in *A Midsummer Night's Dream*. This wood contains mounds upon which the wild thyme grows. Tradition says, moreover, that Shakespeare having been apprehended by two Grendon constables for some small misdemeanour (probably that of having slept a night in the church porch), and resenting the charge of sturdy beggardom, immortalized the two men, superbly and not wholly with malice, as Dogberry and Verges, twin redoubtables of the Watch.

Grendon Church should be visited, for it contains traces

of medieval murals, and a fine Jacobean pulpit. Early
Decorated merges with Early English, for those who can
perceive and relish such matters.

From Grendon you must now turn eastward, down the
high street, for about 200 yards, taking a footpath to the
left just before Pear Tree Farm, which stands on the
opposite side of the road.

This path continues south-east for a mile and a half,
across sequestered meadows, over a by-lane, past Ovinghill
Farm and Binwell Lane Farm, leaving the hamlet of Woodham on your right.   The footpath leaps four small brooks,
and at the fourth, immediately before the railway at Waddesdon Road Station, it turns sharply right, crosses the Akeman
Way once more, and continues to the inn at Wescott, at
which point (and in deference to the wishes of generations
of Englishmen) it shows no desire to continue, and in fact
comes to a sudden halt, and is to be seen no more.

Wescott is a small overbuilt hamlet, so called because it
lies to the west of the parent village of Waddesdon.   Philosophy Farm, here, is interesting for its name.

At the eastern end of Wescott you follow an old track
leftward.   It becomes a footpath and climbs gently for
about one mile, with Waddesdon Manor Woods away to
the right.   At length it brings you into Waddesdon, once
more beside the inn.

Waddesdon is not a beautiful village, yet it possesses a
neat charm of its own, very proper to a village that became
the property of a Duke of Marlborough.   It puts one in
mind of a similar ducal decency at Woburn, seat of the
Bedfordshire Russells.   It is Waddesdon, incidentally, that
provides us with a clue to Philosophy Farm's academic
name, that Squeers-like blend of the practical with the
theoretical, for in 1618 a certain Sir William Sedley,
Knight and Baronet, bequeathed the sum of £200 to endow

a lecture in natural philosophy at the University of Oxford, the said sum being invested in lands near Waddesdon. Philosophy Farm, in short, represents the "four yard-lands and four acres" that were bequeathed to the lecturer for ever.

From Waddesdon the motor-buses will take you into Bicester or Aylesbury, each town being on a main railway line.

If you wish to continue for a few miles, you will be well advised to make for Quainton. The best way thither lies along the right-hand lane out of Waddesdon, in the direction of Bicester, from which, after a few hundred yards, a footpath forks right, and leads directly into Quainton, having crossed the railway mid-way between Waddesdon Road and Quainton Road Station. (The name "Road" when applied to a railway station is a sure sign that the place and the station stand a very considerable distance apart, as at Bodmin, down in Cornwall.)

Soon after crossing the track, your way leaps a small stream and proceeds toward Quainton. Magnificent views are open to you from this path. On your right, half ahead, you will see the hill village of Oving, more than 500 feet above sea-level; and on your left, where the railway branches into two tracks, Finemere Wood is visible on a high ridge. From Quainton Hill, which is more than 700 feet up, and stands immediately north of the village, you will have a clear view across the Vale of Aylesbury, whence the Chilterns stand against the skyline. From this place their contours are clearly discernible—the slight dip in the centre, and the high promontories above Whiteleaf and by Combe Hill, which is not far short of 1,000 feet high.

Quainton is a delightful spot and an historic spot, and it will please you. Its owner at the time of Domesday was a Norman, Milo Crispin. The manor passed during the

WOMAN AND
WINE,
QUAINTON

THE VILLAGE
GREEN,
QUAINTON

later Middle Ages to Thomas de Missenden, who took his name from Great and Little Missenden, Chiltern villages of great charm and beauty, twenty miles away, on the other side of the Whiteleaf escarpment. For a time also the manor was held by the great Verney family, of Steeple Claydon, a few miles to the east. In the centre of the village a stone cross was erected by the Knights Hospitallers, according to tradition, but the argument is by analogy only—similar crosses are found elsewhere, known to have been erected by the Knights—and cannot be accepted with certainty.

The soil around Quainton will interest the amateur geologist: first, and in a lesser vein, because a fine meadow in the south-east of the village was at one time a well-known race-course; and secondly because the fields to the north of the place contain many sands of different colours. Limestone quarries were dug here in earlier times, and these abound in fossils. After a heavy shower of rain it is possible to unearth many stones and fossils merely by stirring the topsoil with a walking-stick.

I advise a visit to the summit of the high ground north of Quainton, 786 feet above the sea, whence, on a clear day, and with the help of good glasses, the Welsh mountains can be seen. This view differs from those to be had from the Chilterns. Chiltern views possess a more intimate loveliness. More often than not they open only so far as the next ridge, to reveal deep combes and chalky bottoms, havens of unknown solitude, with sometimes a blue wisp of smoke sidling skyward from a hidden cottage or farm; but the vista from Quainton Hill is wider. It lacks the intimacy and cup-like symmetry of a typical Chiltern view—say, for instance, from Christmas Common, or looking down deep into Bix Bottom—and at the same time it has a sweep beyond the range of narrow valley and

K

interlocking spur.   It is worth while, I think, to climb the hill out of Quainton, and to gaze across England into Wales.

And when you have seen Wales, and thought your thoughts thereon, you will find at Quainton a railway and a motor-bus to carry you into Aylesbury.

CHAPTER EIGHT

FROM ROWSHAM AND ASTON ABBOTS, THROUGH STEWKLEY
AND DRAYTON PARSLOW, TO THE TWO HORWOODS.
(ABOUT 12 MILES)

FROM Aylesbury take the motor-bus along the Leighton
Buzzard road to Rowsham, a distance of four miles.

From the inn at Rowsham proceed through the village
until you reach the barns on the right of the road, the
last buildings in the village. Across the road from these
you will find a gate and a footpath leading directly up
the meadow, parallel with the road at first, but soon veering
leftward away from it.

At the top of this hill you have uninterrupted views
across the Vale of Aylesbury, with the Chilterns on the skyline, stretching visible from the Hertfordshire border to the
Oxfordshire border, from Tring to Chinnor.

You will pass a farm on your right, and afterwards a
covert—Fox Covert—very neat and circular, on your left.
A short climb once again will take you into the village of
Aston Abbots, a picturesque place despite one or two
council houses. Aston House, here, was the country seat
of the Abbots of Saint Albans, but at the Dissolution passed
to the Earls of Chesterfield. The Church of Saint James
has many notable features—the plain Norman porch will
strike you as you enter, and, inside, the intricate Decorated
piscina in the chancel's south wall. Most moving also,
when last I went there, was the list of villagers who had
served in the two late wars. It is a fine thought that
throughout the breadth of England, in many of her churches,
are emblazoned the names of her country folk, some of them
of great renown, others, the majority, utterly unknown

beyond their hamlet, who have died, or been wounded, or returned unscathed out of the man-made inferno. There, to the curious gaze, are the ancient gentry, the officers of famous regiments; and there also, often not less ancient, the Hodges and the Biggs and the Perks, redoubtable privates, impassive sergeants, or seamen to the manner born, who from their native fields went out to the splendour of the East, or to the rigours of the North, or to the fearful challenge of the grey seas. *Vere requiescant in pace.*

By the white houses near the church you will find a foot-path leading through many remote fields. It leaps a brook by means of one plank, and leaves Westpark Farm on its right. Just beyond the copse on the left, over the brow of a hill, you turn sharp left into a field and carry across the by-lane from Wing to Cublington. To-day, unfortunately, this route entails some steering among R.A.F. encampments, but the way can be found, and, when found, is delightful.

You begin to climb here, to nearly 500 feet, with the tower of Wing Church gleaming behind you, and once more a view leftward of the extreme tip of the Chilterns above Chinnor. At the farm by North Cottlesloe you cross a grassy track, and afterwards a small stream—again by means of one plank—until at length you pass Warren Farm and enter the southern end of Stewkley, with signpost to guide you along the quarter-mile into the centre of the village.

For an hour you have been walking among isolated fields, and in Stewkley you come upon a village that also is not noticeably connected with the rest of the world.

In 1066 *Stiuclai*—so called from the stiff-clay of the soil—was held by three men, the Bishop of Constance, Milo Crispin, and Walter Giffard, all of them Normans. For the next two centuries the lands were variously distributed by the King among his relatives and favourites. At Pitch Green, which stands about 600 yards from the church, and is said to have been the scene of a fierce skirmish during the Civil Wars, many skulls and bones have been ploughed up. From this spot you have views south-east to the three Brickhills.

The Church of Saint Michael is a unique instance of early Norman architecture, and has sometimes been called Saxon, though it evidently bears close resemblance to many other churches that are known to have been built by the early Normans. The place at all events deserves, and will amply repay, careful study. The Roundheads, after the fashion of Phillistines, converted the chancel of Stewkley Church into a stables. There is a pleasing custom, observed each Christmas, of strewing the floor of the church with fresh straw that was at one time provided by tenants of tithe land in the village. This custom they called " littering ".

From Stewkley to Drayton Parslow is a winding country road that descends slightly to the hamlet of North End, but rises again as it enters Drayton Parslow, 500 feet up. All along the way you have splendid views—eastward to the Brickhills, with the canal glittering at their feet; south-east to Oving and the three Claydons; south-west, distant and blue, the Chilterns. You may even be able to make out the trees of Christmas Gorse, four miles to the south-west, on the far side of the Aylesbury–Winslow highway.

In order to enter Drayton Parslow you must turn right for a few hundred yards at Potash Farm. This manor belonged once to the Conqueror's half-brother, Odo of Bayeaux, that notable medieval landowner, and for many centuries afterwards was the property of the Fortescues. In the last century it was purchased by the Earl of Carrington.

The church here is worth notice, having survived some drastic restoration during the Victorian era. By removing

A BY-WAY IN WINSLOW

WING CHURCH, FROM THE GATEWAY

the drugget you may see the remains of several sixteenth-century brasses.

From this sleepy village make your way along a sleepy lane, through the hamlet of Mursley, to a place where the road forks left into Little Horwood, and right towards Whaddon. A few yards along the Horwood route, and on the right of the lane, strike a footpath that will lead you over the railway and by an aqueduct, and at length, bearing left by a copse, into the hamlet of Little Horwood.

This small gathering of homesteads is north Buckinghamshire at its most remote. Scarcely a cottage in the village is without some pleasing feature, and most of them are thatched and timbered and whitewashed. Little Horwood was not mentioned in the Domesday Survey, but one supposes that it was joined, and surveyed, with Winslow, a few miles to the south-west. For many years the manor belonged to the Fortescues, by whom it was sold, in the seventeenth century, to George Villiers, at that time a Knight, whose son sold it to the Selby-Lowndes of Whaddon.

The rectory is a fine mansion, some way from the church, and it is interesting to recall that Queen Victoria used to receive a supply of fresh butter from a dairy in the village, the butter being despatched, every day, to Buckingham Palace.

The Church of Saint Nicholas is locked during the week, but I advise you to visit the place if you happen to be there on a Sunday or during service hour. It has a musicians' gallery, erected in 1787. Readers of *Under the Greenwood Tree* will recall, what is commonly overlooked, that the organ, often the most hideous feature of English parish churches, is relatively a modern innovation; singing, in the past, having been either unaccompanied, or accompanied by the fiddles, flutes, and viols of musicians in the gallery.

SUMMER-TIME NEAR STOKE HAMMOND

At Little Horwood you are in the heart of the Whaddon Chase country, perhaps the most remote and unsullied in Buckinghamshire, certainly typical of this part of the County. The farming, as you observe, is largely for milk and for the roots that feed a herd. The land being relatively low, is well watered and offers first-rate pasturage for sheep and cattle.

From Little Horwood, meanwhile, your way leads to Great Horwood, along twenty minutes of narrow winding lane. As you leave the hamlet—its church and ancient inn on the right—you will see a magnificent old timbered house, standing a little to the left of the lane, and, after that, a division of the ways: one turning going rightward to Whaddon; the other leftward, to our destination, Great Horwood.

The lane starts to climb again hereabouts until it reaches

652 feet, and at the top of a rise, where the way bends slightly right and left, you will notice a perfect example of modest Elizabethan domestic architecture—a small cottage standing alone on the right of the road. Fortunate indeed were the men to whom this was home. I have passed this isolated homestead several times, and upon each occasion I stood fascinated, trying to analyse what it is in these old buildings that seizes upon the imagination, and delights the senses, and altogether makes the houses of our own time seem vulgarly mediocre. Is it, I ask myself, the merely sentimental appeal of times past ? Am I asking, with Villon, " *Ou sont les neiges d'antan*? " I think not, for the relics of Norman castles, that also are old, and older indeed than this house, though they stir the historic imagination, do not delight the aesthetic sense. Partly, I think, the charm of this cottage, and of its many fellows, lies in the abundance of what I can only call the features of its face. A typical modern house, even of the better sort, is after all a flat and too-polished affair, its *façade* an opaque space relieved (or gashed) by regular slots for door and window, its flanks or backside draped by the unlovely *appanages* of sanitation. In a Tudor house, on the contrary, nothing is flat or polished. The face is indeed a face, and the impression of its humanity made more lively by thatch, which may be compared with a cap or with a fringe of golden hair draped over the eyes. Then, too, the timbers and rafters, criss-crossing the brick or white stone, deceive the sensitive eye into mistaking them for furrows that Time has planted thereon, after his well-known fashion, proofs that a heart has lived and loved and most fully had its being. Closer inspection—unless a man is too scientific to accept the existence of psychic reality—closer inspection, I suggest, reveals humanity in the window panes, their lozenge glass or mullioned eyebrows seeming very face-like indeed

ANCIENT AND MODERN AT STEWKLEY

—darker, no doubt, than our present sun-ray devices, yet in winter more snug, and cooler through summer. How utterly delightful also, and quite beyond the power of words to describe them, are those infinite small windows that peep like kind eyes beneath tufts of eyebrows, the eyebrows being in this instance the fringe of the thatch. And when at length you enter in to the hall, and feel the strong flags sure under your feet, and the rich dark rafters massive through the walls, surely you have scant patience with those people who would barter these things for linoleum and the glib joys of central heating. It may be, of course, that a lifetime of urban comfort has so softened and unmade a man that he cannot delight in these older charms, being slave to his electric toaster, and lackey to those electric fires that have in them an imitation flame—without doubt the most subtle perversion to which the times have yet lured us. If, on the other hand, he has had the good fortune to live and to be bred in a house such as this, the newer ways of progress will appal him, and, heavy with the hope deferred that maketh the heart sick, he will long for the bulges and the windings and the dark corners of the old home, and will find in all other features only the slick consolations that are not consolations, and the progress that is not progress, and the devices that are not devices at all, but only bad habits that take the verve from endeavour and the zest from achievement. As I look at this cottage, I ask, with Elia, " Antiquity, thou wondrous charm, what art thou? that, being nothing, art everything! When thou wert, thou wert not antiquity—then thou wert nothing, but hadst a remoter antiquity, as thou calledst it, to look back to with blind veneration; thou thyself being to thyself flat, jejeune, *modern*! "

I find that my thoughts have been expressed for me in poetry:

> Let there remain in England, in these hills,
> some few old homes whose water is the well,
> whose lamps burn oil, whose beverage is beer,
> let there remain, along with me on earth
> some ancient few who yet prefer to walk,
> to whom the trinket toys of luxury,
> spewed out by commerce for commercial gain,
> are hostages to fortune, and no more.

These, at any rate, are stray thoughts that you may care to meditate as you walk along this peaceful lane into Great Horwood, whose greatness, I may add, is decidedly a relative greatness, the village itself being uncommonly small and off the beaten track.

On the outskirts of this village—and fortunately so— your way will be made offensive to you by a bijou estate of red council houses, modernity's common ailment, for which no cure exists, since the ailment is not nowadays considered to be such, but rather is counted a blessing, and proof of the nation's economic well-being.

Having passed these, however, you will enter upon the true spirit of the place, which is made manifest by magni-

ficent cottages, all of them carefully tended, evidently the homes of persons who care for them because they love them. The lane opens on to a green, the green being very small, and the opening very great—with an inn that cannot escape notice, and many more old homes. The church stands a little onward, to the right of the road, just this side of the cross-roads.

Great Horwood (or Horwood Magna, or Horwood-cum-Singleborough, or Hereworde) was presented by Walter Giffard, Earl of Buckingham, to the Priors of Newton Longeville, who were suppressed in 1415, and their lands then granted to John, Duke of Bedford, on whose death it passed to the Warden and Scholars of New College, Oxford. The College used to hold a court-leet and a court-baron here every year.

It seems difficult to believe that this small and drowsy village, slightly behind the back-of-beyond, was at one time a flourishing centre of trade; yet Henry VI granted to New College the right to hold a weekly market here, and a fair each year, at the Feast of Saint James—on the day before, the day of, and the day after, the Feast.

Great Horwood has a sinister claim upon our attention, for it was once noted as a plague centre. In September of 1858 a form of typhoid fever broke out here. It lasted for nearly twelve months, and baffled the best doctors in the Kingdom. London newspapers sent reporters to investigate and the name of Great Horwood became known throughout the land as the " Fever Village ". The Regius

JANUARY MORNING NEAR GREAT HORWOOD

Professor of Medicine in the University of Oxford, a Dr. Ackland, who was invited to draw up his report on the matter, found that one inhabitant in six succumbed to the plague, and that one in seven of the victims was killed by it.

The Professor's report, incidentally, contains a description of the village that is worth repeating in order to show how slightly the place has changed during the past hundred years. The village, he says, " occupies a ridge of the oolite which runs down from Whaddon Chase in a westerly direction, is bounded on either side by a moderate valley, and terminates by a gentle fall a mile to the south-west of the township (*sic*). In each valley a small rivulet runs, generally from east to west; the two rivulets unite at the east of the slope just named, and the joint stream enters the Ouse between Padbury and Buckingham.   There is, therefore, a natural fall to the north, the south, and the west.   The parish is pleasantly but not excessively wooded, grows splendid corn, and has meadows of rich pasture on undulating slopes."   The villagers, he adds, are hard-working and clean, and many of the young girls earn so much as sixteen shillings a week by making lace at home.   That would be the equivalent of at least five pounds a week to-day.

The church is a notable specimen of Decorated work, having many features unscathed by restoration or the Roundheads.   One of its rectors was William Warham, Bishop of London, and Primate of All England, in the reign of Henry VII.

It is sad that the unique custom of " Stephening ", which

BETWEEN THE HORWOODS

A WELCOME SIGHT IN ASTON ABBOTS

used to be observed here and at Drayton Parslow, has been allowed to lapse with the times; though I understand that a movement to start a grass-track for motor-cycle racing in the neighbourhood enjoys wide support. This good old English custom took place upon Saint Stephen's Day, when the parishioners assembled at the Rectory, there to consume as much bread and cheese, and to drink as much good ale as they could, at the rector's expense. One rector, Basil Woodd—the spelling is his own, not mine—discovered (what cannot have needed much experience to perceive) that this custom caused some riotness. Instead of so limiting the ale as to obviate the disturbance, Mr. Woodd discontinued the practice, and commuted the victuals for cash. In 1827 he went one worse, and discontinued the cash. In 1834 the Charity Commissioners were asked to restore the custom. They replied that they could not

find the origin of its usage, nor any legal obligation upon
the rector to provide the meal.   Thus passed another good
old English custom.

Nevertheless, not every English squire has retired bankrupt
and bewildered beneath the burden of taxation, for when
last I passed this way, on a golden evening of late September,
I met a real old-fashioned harvest-home.   It was only a
symbolic pageant, but it sufficed to cheer my heart and to
stir my imagination.   Perched high upon the crusty stooks
in a gay blue-and-red wain, a little girl rode as Queen of
the Harvest, her yellow hair bound by a pink ribbon.   The
old horse (dressed by his carter) jangled and jingled and
blazed with brass bright in the sunset.   Two or three
women, and a dozen hands, marched alongside, and, as
they marched, a motor shooting-brake drew up, and the
farmer's wife began to serve beer from a barrel, and home-
made pies.   It did the heart good to see that at least one
Englishman had not forgotten the

> Lord of the Harvest riding home in state
> to harvest suppers capped with ale or mead
> or golden cider frothy in the pot,
> when all the village (children, maids, and crones
> the cobbler, tailor, baker, and the priest)
> came forth to bring September's harvest home.

From Great Horwood to Winslow is not above half an
hour's walk by the road; or, if you prefer to wait, you may
find a motor-bus; but I am not certain that these run every
day.   At Winslow you will find another bus, or a train, to
carry you to Aylesbury.

And here, in the very heart of northern Buckinghamshire, we must take leave of one another, and go our ways.
You have, as I hope, ranged among some of the deepest and
sturdiest country in southern England; and if—as, also, I
hope—you are good English folk, or proud Britons, you

L

THE REMOTE FARMSTEAD NEAR MURSLEY

will take your part in the preservation of that country. It is a solemn reflection, that if one man in ten thousand were to stand forth as the champion of the English countryside, making his voice heard and his message respected, then the majority might be powerless to sully the landscape, for one man who cares is worth ten thousand who do not care. If one man in ten thousand were to keep watch over his own village—not officiously or pedantically, but with the just eye of reasonableness—and were to protest strongly, vehemently, and with persistence, against all attempts to despoil the scene—if such a man were to arise, then petrol pumps would be concealed, or so contrived as not to offend, as now they offend; cinemas would be built discreetly, or put among back streets, whence they did not obtrude;

houses would be set up indeed for the work-people, but houses that were homes of a modest distinction, made, if that were possible, of a local stone, not set down and flung up willy-nilly by idle bureaucrats in rigid ranks of unseemly blankness.

Then, too, under the guidance of that small ten-thousandth, common good manners would be observed in the matter of omnibus halts, advertisement hoardings, and the disposition of such things as gas works, refuse dumps, and other symbols of civic life.   Nor would the matter end there, for the zealous ten-thousandth among us would ensure that no footpath were curtailed nor diverted nor closed without just cause.   These, I hear it said, are small enough ills in a nation that is just now fighting for its mere existence; but man never yet has lived fully on a diet of bread alone, and there is no profit to him if, in winning the world's markets, he loses his own soul.   By their fruits shall ye know them.   A people that forgets its national heritage, or besmirches it with all manner of grotesque ugliness, is a barren tree, that needs not to be cut down nor cast into the fiery furnace, for it will fall soon enough, and perish of its own corruption.

And, finally, on no account think this a matter for others to undertake—a problem beyond the scope of any one man to solve.   That way lies dictatorship and the *malaise* of a too-literal democracy.   On the contrary, here is a matter—and of momentous import and urgency—to which every man and woman can attend.   There are many fronts on which this battle is to be won, or lost—in Parliament, in the Press, upon local councils, and in private conversation. You are, I take it, democrats—that is to say, people who dislike being regimented by Orders in Council and by mediocre bureaucrats.   Very well then; exert on behalf of your own countryside, and for your children's sake, one tenth part of the cunning and persistence that you employed to increase your dividends or to enlarge your pay-packet. Our countryside is to be saved, not by the exertions of one man, but by the exertions of every man. It is a battle in which you will be creating, not destroying; conserving, not squandering; a battle in which you will fight side by side with your fellows and on their behalf; a great bloodless (but how bitter) revolution against what is ugly, and incongruous, and merely useful.

There are no more worlds for us to conquer. Our conquering days are done. We have fought twice to save a thankless world, and we have emerged, victorious indeed, but mortally wounded, and with our tail for ever knotted into submission. Unlike Alexander, we need not weep, for there is one small island still left for us to conquer; and its name is England. For the past century we have despoiled and defiled it. Unable ever again to conquer others, let us now conquer ourselves.

Prestwood,
1947–8.

INDEX